New Headway
Culture and Literature Companion

Elementary

Christopher Barker
Libby Mitchell

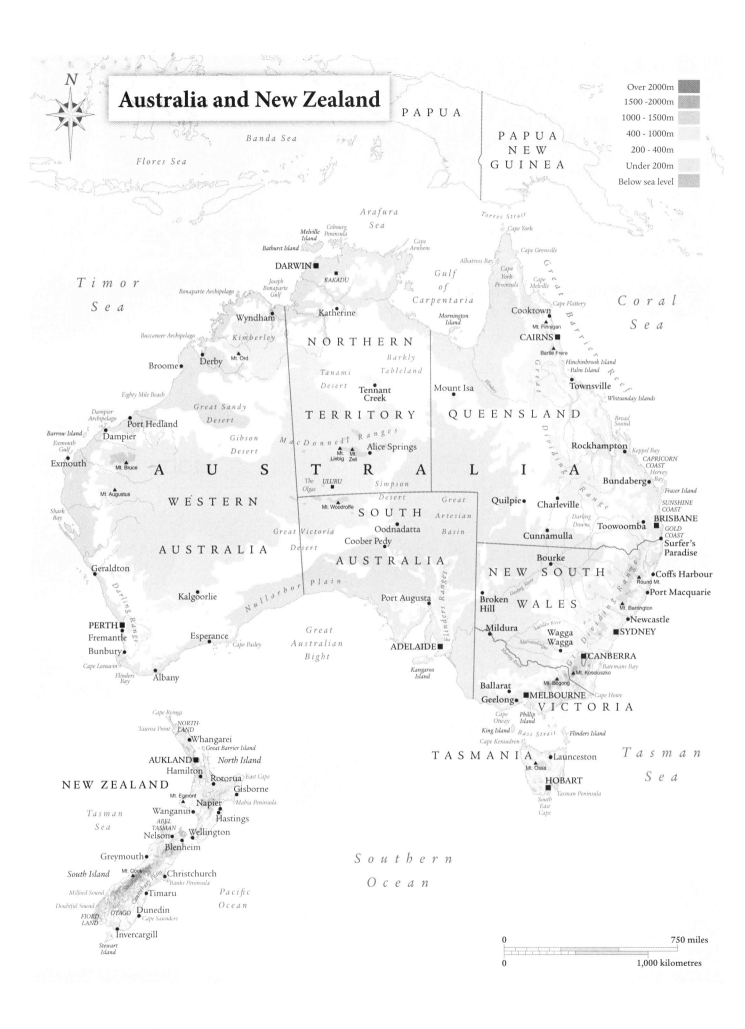

Contents

		Map of the British Isles	Inside Front Cover
		Maps of Australia and New Zealand	p2
1	Culture	Countries in the UK	p4
2	Culture	Great British Food	p6
3	Culture	Halloween	p8
4	Culture	Bonfire Night	p10
5	Culture	Christmas around the world	p12
6	Culture	Hogmanay	p14
7	Culture	Pantomime	p16
8	Culture	An English village	p18
9	Culture	Two schools in India and Pakistan	p20
10	Culture	February Festivals	p22
11	Culture	A nice cup of tea	p24
12	Culture	A walk through London	p26
13	Culture	Robin Hood – England's most famous folk hero	p28
14	Culture	New Zealand	p30
15	Literature	Roger McGough – *Mafia Cats*	p32
16	Literature	Mark Twain – *The Adventures of Tom Sawyer*	p34
17	Literature	Wendy Cope – Three poems	p36
18	Literature	Oscar Wilde – *The Canterville Ghost*	p38
19	Literature	John Cooper Clarke – *I wanna be yours*	p40
20	Literature	Bram Stoker – *Dracula*	p42
		Glossary	p44
		Map of USA and Canada	Inside Back Cover

1

CULTURE

Countries in the UK

1 Try and answer the questions before you look at the texts.

1 Which has more countries in it – the United Kingdom (UK) or Great Britain (GB)?

2 Match the countries and capital cities:

1 England	a Cardiff
2 Scotland	b London
3 Wales	c Belfast
4 Northern Ireland	d Edinburgh

3 Which has the higher population, Scotland or Wales?

4 Do people in the UK use the euro?

5 How many official languages are there in the United Kingdom?

2

Which is worth more, one pound or one euro?

3 Look at the examples of English, Welsh, Scots Gaelic, and Cornish in the table.

1 Welsh and Cornish use the same word for 'good'. What is it?

2 In Scots Gaelic and Cornish, what are the words for 'morning'?

3 In Welsh, what is the word for 'you'?

4 In Welsh and Scots Gaelic, what are the words for 'and'?

4 Were your answers to the questions in Exercise 1 correct?

FACT FILE

Britain, Great Britain	United Kingdom
= England, Scotland, Wales	= England, Scotland, Wales, Northern Ireland

POPULATION

United Kingdom total is 60.6 million.

83.8% live in England.

8.4% live in Scotland.

4.9% live in Wales.

2.9% live in Northern Ireland.

OFFICIAL LANGUAGES OF THE UK	
Main language	Minority languages
English	Welsh (Wales) Gaelic (Ireland, Scotland) Cornish (Cornwall)

English	Welsh	Scots Gaelic	Cornish
Good morning!	Bore da!	Madainn mhath!	Myttin da!
How are you?	Sut rydych chi?	Ciamar a tha thu?	Fatla genes?
Very well, thanks.	Da iawn, diolch.	Tha gu math, tapadh leat.	Yn poynt da, meur rasta.
And you?	A chi?	Agus thusa?	Ha ty?

Headway Culture and Literature Companion Elementary

5 Read the text. Then write the names of the places under the photos.

Places to visit

Start your visit in London. First, go on the London Eye. It's a big wheel. Take some photos from the top. You can see all over London.

The Romans in Britain? Well, they're not there now, but in Bath you can see the beautiful Roman baths. The city is good for shops, too. But don't spend all your money at the shops. It costs £6.80 (if you are under 16) to visit the Roman baths.

Take a train to Newquay in Cornwall. Spend a whole day surfing, swimming and relaxing on the beach. The average temperature in August is 16°C, so it's not too hot and not too cold. The train journey from London takes five hours.

Climb Mount Snowdon in north Wales. It's 1085 metres high. If you want to go higher, try Ben Nevis in Scotland (1343 metres), the highest mountain in the UK.

Visit Edinburgh and walk along the Royal Mile, from Edinburgh Castle to the Palace of Holyrood House, through the medieval heart of Edinburgh. But don't expect to see the Queen at the Castle or the Palace. When she's in Scotland, she stays at Balmoral, a castle surrounded by forests and rivers.

UK

Edinburgh Castle

in Wales

_____   _____   _____

6a Write the words and phrases under the correct heading.

| Roman baths   ~~shops~~   ~~national parks~~   surfing |
| forests   mountains   palaces   restaurants   relaxing on the beach |
| castles   rivers   swimming |

Facilities	Beach life	Buildings	Landscape and scenery
shops			
national parks			

6b *spend* and *take*

spend

You can *spend* money, but you can also *spend* time.

Find an example of each in the text.

take

Find three uses of the verb *take* in the text.

What do you think?

▸ Look again at the information on these pages. Is there anything that surprises you?

It surprises me that ... (there are more than 60 million people in the UK).

▸ Look at the words and phrases in Exercise 6a. On holiday, which things are important for you?

I like going to places where you can walk in the mountains.

I enjoy spending all day at the beach and I love surfing.

▸ You're planning to go to the UK for a week. Where would you like to go, and why?

I want to go to ... because ...
I'd like to go to ...

What about you? Where do you want to go?

PROJECT

Design a leaflet or a web page for someone visiting your country. Use these headings as a guide:
- Population
- Languages
- Money
- Places to visit

2

CULTURE
Great British Food

1 Match the dishes with the countries.

1 Italy	a curry
2 Spain	b moussaka
3 Turkey	c pizza
4 Greece	d paella
5 Japan	e kebab
6 India	f sushi

2 Read the text and write the numbers of the dishes in the pictures.

The Top Ten Great British Dishes

Italian, Indian, Thai, Chinese, Japanese, Greek, Turkish ... you can find all these kinds of food everywhere in Britain. When you go out for a meal, get a takeaway or buy ready meals from the supermarket, it's likely to be curry, pizza, sushi, or kebabs. So what is British food? And do people still eat it?

In fact, you can find traditional British food in Britain today. Most pubs serve traditional dishes and some people cook them at home. So here are the top ten favourites, according to a survey by UKTV.

[1]

1 ROAST BEEF AND YORKSHIRE PUDDING
Roast beef and Yorkshire Pudding* is the classic Sunday lunch. You usually eat it with roast potatoes, mashed potatoes, vegetables and gravy (juice from the meat made into a sauce). Variations include roast lamb with mint sauce, roast pork with apple sauce, and roast chicken.
* The ingredients of Yorkshire Pudding are flour, milk and eggs. You eat it with the meat, or as a starter, with gravy, before the meat.

2 FISH AND CHIPS
This is the original British takeaway food. It's fresh fish fried in batter (a mixture of flour and milk), with thick chips. You usually put salt and vinegar on the chips.

3 STEAK AND KIDNEY PIE
A pie has pastry on the top and may have it on the bottom, too. To make steak and kidney pie, you cut beef and kidney into pieces and cook them slowly. Then you cover the mixture with pastry and bake it.

4 SHEPHERD'S PIE
It's called Shepherd's pie because it's made of minced lamb. It doesn't have pastry on top; it has mashed potato.

5 CULLEN SKINK
This is a Scottish smoked fish soup, made with potatoes and onions.

6 SAUSAGE AND MASH
This dish is sometimes called 'bangers and mash'. (Sausages can explode – go BANG! – when you fry or grill them, which is why people sometimes call them 'bangers'). It's mashed potato with sausages and gravy.

7 COOKED BREAKFAST
The traditional 'full English breakfast' is bacon, eggs, sausages, tomatoes, baked beans, and fried bread. People don't often eat it at home, except on Sundays, but it is popular in cafés (especially those on motorways and near where people are working in manual jobs).

8 RHUBARB AND CUSTARD
Rhubarb is a plant with tall pink or red stems. You cook it and eat it with custard, a mixture of eggs, milk and sugar.

9 FISH PIE
This is another pie without pastry, like Shepherd's pie. It's a mixture of fish in a creamy sauce with mashed potato on top.

10 TRIFLE
Trifle is for special occasions. It's a dessert of fruit, such as strawberries and raspberries, and pieces of sponge cake covered in custard and cream. In Italy there's a similar dessert called *zuppa inglese*, which means 'English soup'!

Headway Culture and Literature Companion Elementary

3 Which is the odd one out? Explain your choice.

1 Steak and kidney pie   Shepherd's pie   Fish pie

   Steak and kidney pie, because it has pastry on top. The other two have mashed potato on top.
   Fish pie, because it's made of fish. The other two are made of meat.

2 Fish pie   Sausage and mash   Trifle

   _____

3 Cullen skink   Fish pie   Fish and chips

   _____

4 Rhubarb and custard   Trifle   Steak and kidney pie

   _____

5 Roast beef and Yorkshire pudding   Roast lamb and mint sauce   Shepherd's pie

   _____

4a Match the adjectives with the pictures.

| 1 roast | 2 mashed | 3 fried | 4 minced | 5 smoked |

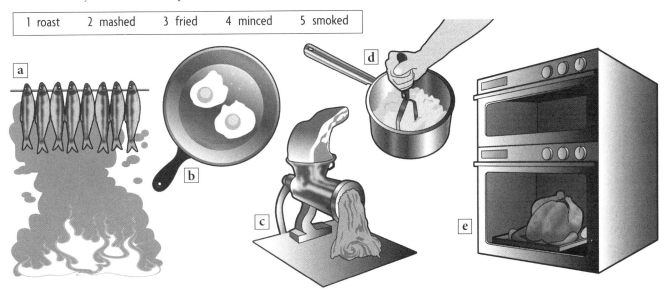

4b Find items in the text to put in each column.

meat	fruit and vegetables	sauces
beef	potatoes	gravy

What do you think?

▶ What are the top ten dishes in your country? In groups, make a list. Then discuss your choices as a class.

▶ Compare your top ten dishes with the top ten British dishes. Are there any which are similar?

PROJECT

Write a short description of your top ten dishes for an English website called 'Top 10 dishes around the world'. Use the descriptions of the 'Top Ten Great British Dishes' as a model.

3

CULTURE

Halloween

1 Answer the questions.
  1 Do you celebrate Halloween (31st October) in your country? If so, what happens?
  2 What do you know about the origins of Halloween?
  3 What do you know about Halloween in other countries?
  4 Can you think of any references to Halloween in books, films or TV programmes?

2 Read the text about Halloween.

ghost

(1) When is Halloween?
Halloween is celebrated on 31st October, the day before All Saints' Day. The word 'Halloween' is from 'All Hallow Even'. 'Even' is short for 'evening'. 'Hallow' means 'sacred', 'holy' or 'saint'. So Halloween is the holy evening before All Saints' Day.

(2)
The ancient Celtic festival of Samhain (/seuɪn/ meaning 'Summer's End'), at the beginning of November, marked the end of the farming season and the beginning of winter. The Celts (the early inhabitants of Britain) believed that on the evening before Samhain, the summer sun god passes into the world of the dead. Because the door between the two worlds is open, it is a good time for supernatural creatures and the spirits of the dead to revisit their former homes and help the living. The visit was welcomed, and families put an extra place at the dinner table for dead relatives.

(3)
Many of the things people do at Halloween reflect its Celtic past. For example, the Celts dressed in costumes and masks to mix with the spirits of the dead. Today we are more afraid that the dead will come back in order to scare us, and people dress as ghosts and devils at Halloween. Other costumes include skeletons, witches, vampires, werewolves and mummies.

(4)
Many of the modern Halloween traditions began in America, and are now popular in Britain and other English-speaking countries. The most popular Halloween activity is 'trick or treating'. Children dress up as witches or ghosts and go to their neighbours' houses. They knock on the door and say: "Trick or treat?" Their neighbours give them a treat, for example, some chocolate or some sweets; if not, the children play a trick on them, like throwing eggs at the windows.

(5)
It's traditional to tell ghost stories and to show scary films at Halloween, such as *Dracula*, *The Wolf Man* and the *Halloween* films. One of the most recent references to Halloween is in the Harry Potter books, where it is an important date for magic. Halloween also features in films such as *The Nightmare Before Christmas*, *Monster House*, *Donnie Darko*, *Hocus Pocus*, and *The Halloween That Almost Wasn't*. TV specials for Halloween include: *The Worst Witch*, *The Simpsons: Treehouse of Horror* and *It's the Great Pumpkin, Charlie Brown*

(6)
- You light a candle in a dark room. If it flickers and then turns blue, it means there is a spirit in the room.
- You peel an apple in one long piece and throw the apple peel over your shoulder. The peel lands in the shape of the first letter of your future husband's or wife's name.

(7)
pumpkin lanterns   black cats   bats   owls   spiders

It's traditional to make a pumpkin lantern for Halloween. You use a knife to take out the inside of a pumpkin and cut the shapes of eyes, a nose and a mouth. Then you put a candle inside it. You put the pumpkin outside your house to keep the bad spirits away.

(8)
Orange symbolises: autumn, the leaves changing colour, harvest, fire, pumpkins, sunset.
Black symbolises: death, evil, winter, night, witches, black cats, bats.

3 Read the text again and write these headings in the correct places.
a) Colours of Halloween
b) Halloween in books and films
c) Halloween today across the world
d) Symbols of Halloween
e) Why do people wear strange costumes at Halloween?
f) Two old Halloween customs
g) When is Halloween? *1*
h) What are the origins of Halloween?

4 Write questions for these answers:

1 *What does 'Halloween' mean?*
It means 'holy evening'.

2 _____
It was an ancient Celtic festival.

3 _____
Because they wanted the spirits of the dead to feel welcome.

4 _____
They dress up and go 'trick or treating'.

5 _____
Because it's an important date for magic.

6 _____
It means there's a spirit in the room, according to an old Halloween custom.

7 _____
To keep bad spirits away.

8 _____
It symbolises autumn and the things associated with it.

5 Use words from the text to label the pictures at the top of the pages.

What do you think?

▸ Choose another festival for which people dress up. Make notes in answer to these questions, then talk about the festival with a friend.

When is it?
Carnival is in (February).

What do people wear?

What do they do?

▸ Australians celebrate Halloween even though October 31st is the start of spring.
Read what two Australians say about Halloween. Then say what you like about your festival.

"It's an excuse to be somebody else for a change, so Halloween is a lot of fun," says Mrs Mathews, the owner of a fancy dress shop.

"I like dressing up and looking pretty or scary. Halloween is about having fun," says Chanise Lumby, 10, dressed as a vampire.

PROJECT

Design a poster for a Halloween party at your school. Include information about costumes, entertainment and competitions.

4

CULTURE

Bonfire Night

1. In Spain, people celebrate the festival of San Juan and midsummer on the night of June 23rd with a big bonfire. Are bonfires part of any celebrations you know about?

2. Read the text about Guy Fawkes.

It's November 5th. It's early evening and all over Britain people are standing around bonfires, either small ones in their gardens, or enormous ones in parks and other public places. In the middle of the bonfire is a guy – a model of a man. He is burning in flames. All around, fireworks are shooting into the night sky. What's going on?

November 5th in Britain is 'Bonfire Night' or 'Guy Fawkes Night'. It is when people remember an event from long ago. Let's go back four hundred years ....

It's 1605. The king of England is James I. He is a Protestant, but there are some Catholics in England who want England to be Catholic.

Guy Fawkes is one of a gang of 13 Catholics, led by Robert Catesby. They plan to put barrels of gunpowder in a cellar below the Houses of Parliament, and blow it up as the king enters on November 5th.

Guy Fawkes' job is to light the gunpowder. He knows a lot about it. He was a soldier with the Spanish army in the Netherlands in the 1590s, trying to make it a Catholic country.

One of the gang, Francis Tresham, sends a letter to his brother-in-law, Lord Monteagle, telling him not to go to Parliament on November 5th. Monteagle is suspicious and gives the letter to the king's men.

The king's men search Parliament. They find Guy Fawkes and arrest him.

3 Match each line of speech to a frame of the cartoon.
1 'Death to the enemy of the king and Parliament!' [6]
2 'There he is! Stop him!' [ ]
3 'Something's wrong. Check everywhere in Parliament!' [ ]
4 'Catesby, Winter, Percy .... Who are the others?' [ ]
5 'Do we all agree? It's time to kill this Protestant king!' [ ]
6 'That's enough to blow up the whole building.' [ ]
7 'Remember, remember the fifth of November...' [ ]

4 Answer the questions.
1 What is a guy? *It's a model of Guy Fawkes.*
2 What do children do with the guy before Bonfire Night?
3 What do they do with the guy on Bonfire Night?
4 Why do adults have to buy the fireworks?
5 What's the difference between a banger and a sparkler?

5a Find words in the text for the following:
1 They're yellow and they come out of a fire. *flames*
2 They're round, wooden, and you keep beer (or gunpowder) in them.
3 A room below a house where you keep things.
4 To cause to explode.
5 A person in the army.
6 Thinking that someone is doing something bad.
7 To take someone's freedom away.
8 To hurt someone to get them to tell you something.
9 Against the law.

5b Notice these uses of the verb *make*:
1 Today, children make a guy, a model of Guy Fawkes.
2 Fireworks which make a loud noise are called 'bangers'.
3 The king's men make Guy Fawkes give the names of the other Catholics.
4 King James makes November 5th an official day of celebration.

How would you translate these sentences into your language? Would the verb be the same in each case?

What do you think?

▶ What do you think about firework celebrations?

I think they're fantastic. I love fireworks and firework displays.

Fireworks are very expensive. I think they're a waste of money – and they're dangerous.

I don't agree. Fireworks are fun. New Year isn't the same without fireworks.

PROJECT

In Britain people have fireworks on Bonfire Night and there's also a big firework display in London at New Year. In China, fireworks play a big part in Chinese New Year celebrations. Write an email to an English friend, describing a celebration involving fireworks in your country.

They torture Guy Fawkes and make him give the names of the other Catholics.

Guy Fawkes is hanged in the gardens of St Paul's Cathedral.

King James makes November 5th an official day of celebration.

Today many British people don't know the history of Bonfire Night, but some children still make a guy, a model of Guy Fawkes, from old clothes. They take the guy around the streets and shout: 'A penny for the guy'. If people give them money, they use it to buy fireworks. An adult buys them, because it's illegal to sell fireworks to children under the age of 18.

Fireworks have colourful names like 'Catherine Wheels', 'Roman Candles' and 'Mount Vesuvius'. Fireworks which shoot into the sky are called 'rockets'; ones which make a loud noise are called 'bangers'; and ones which are safe for children to hold are called 'sparklers'.

5

CULTURE

Christmas around the world

1 Read about Christmas in Spain and Hungary.
  1 Which are the most important days during the Christmas period in Spain and Hungary? What happens on those days?
  2 Which are the most important days in your country?

2 Read about Christmas in the UK and in Australia.

Spain The most important days during the Christmas period are 24th December, when families have a special dinner, and 6th January, when children receive their presents from the Three Kings.

Hungary Mikulás (The Winter Grandfather) comes on 6th December and brings presents for the children. On 24th December, there is a big dinner of fish with rice or potatoes, and pastries. After dinner, the children see the Christmas tree for the first time.

Christmas in the UK

As soon as Halloween and Bonfire Night are over, and often before, the shops are full of things to buy for Christmas. In the weeks before Christmas, people send Christmas cards to their friends and relatives, wishing them a happy Christmas. Most families buy a Christmas tree; they put it in their living room and decorate it with lights and coloured balls. Some people have coloured lights covering the outside of their houses. In cities there are carol singers in the main shopping streets; they collect money for charity. (**1**)

December 24th is called Christmas Eve. It isn't a holiday in the UK but now most people finish work at lunch time and travel to be with their families for the Christmas period. There is no special Christmas Eve meal. People leave presents under the Christmas tree; parents wait until the children have gone to bed before putting the presents under the tree or in a Christmas stocking. (**2**)

On Christmas Day children get up very early to open their presents. Then everybody looks forward to Christmas dinner: roast turkey, with roast potatoes and vegetables, followed by Christmas Pudding. (**3**)

Boxing Day is 26th December. It's a holiday in the UK and a day for sport (mainly horse racing and football) and visiting relatives. The name 'Boxing Day' has nothing to do with boxing. It comes from the time when servants received boxes (small presents) from their employers. Some people still give 'Christmas boxes', for example £5, to their postman/woman or the boy/girl who delivers their newspapers; but they do this in the period just before Christmas, not on Boxing Day. (**4**)

Emily, 15, Australia

Christmas in Australia

"Australia has many of the same Christmas traditions as the UK, but one great difference is that it is summer. I love it! The days are hot and long here. (**5**)

On Christmas Eve, my family and friends go to the Domain, a big park in Sydney, to join in the Carols by Candlelight celebration. We also go for a walk around the neighbourhood when it gets dark to look at all the Christmas lights that people put on their houses. (**6**)

On Christmas Day, my family and I jump into the pool to cool down before going to a relative's house. There we hand out presents and have Christmas lunch. It's too hot to have a hot lunch, so we have a cold lunch of either turkey or seafood. (**7**)"

3 Each sentence ends a paragraph in the texts. Match them with the correct number.

a In the afternoon, we spend the time relaxing in the sun by the pool or having an exciting game of family backyard cricket.

b In villages, they go from house to house to sing. _1_

c On Boxing Day nowadays, the Christmas Sales start in shops and department stores.

d That means you celebrate Christmas in your T-shirt, shorts and flip-flops!

e Then we have our annual photo in front of the Christmas tree with our Santa sacks before going to bed.

f That's because the children believe that Father Christmas comes down the chimney in the night and delivers their presents.

g This is a very rich, heavy mixture containing fruit, nuts and brandy.

4 Find a sentence to describe each picture.

1 _In the weeks before Christmas, people send Christmas cards to their friends and relatives, wishing them a happy Christmas._

5 Look at the texts again. Make a list of all the phrases that contain the word 'Christmas'.

Christmas period   Christmas tree…

What do you think?

▸ What do people tell children about Father Christmas in your country? Is it right to tell children there's a Father Christmas when it's not true?

▸ Is Christmas a happy time for everybody?

PROJECT

Using the text about Christmas in the UK as a model, write to an English friend who is coming to spend Christmas with you, explaining how it is celebrated in your country.

CULTURE
Hogmanay

1. How do you celebrate New Year? In which countries do people celebrate it the most?
2. Read the text about Hogmanay in Scotland.

HOGMANAY

If you want to celebrate New Year in Britain, go to Scotland! In Scotland, New Year's Eve is called 'Hogmanay' and it's the biggest night of the year.

Nobody is really sure where the word 'Hogmanay' comes from but here are some possibilities:

Oige maidne
This means 'new morning' in Old Gaelic, the language of the Scottish Highlands.

Hoguinané
This Norman French word comes from an Old French expression 'Anguillanneuf' meaning 'gift at new year'.

Hoog min dag
This means 'day of great love' in Old Dutch. For centuries the Flemish and Scots were great trading partners, so it's possible that the Scots took the phrase from the Flemish.

Haleg mona
This Old English phrase means 'holy month', meaning the month around Christmas.

The most famous Hogmanay custom is the singing of Auld Lang Syne (from a poem by the Scottish poet Robert Burns). Use the phrases in the box to complete the English version:

- a very hearty drink
- my dear
- old friends
- my trusty friend
- remembered

Auld Lang Syne

Should auld acquaintance be forgot,
And never brought to mind?
Should auld acquaintance be forgot,
And auld lang syne?

Chorus:
For auld lang syne, my jo,
For auld lang syne,
We'll tak' a cup o' kindness yet,
For auld lang syne.

And there's a hand, my trusty fiere,
And gie's a hand o' thine,
And we'll tak a right guid-willie waught,
For auld lang syne!

English version:

Should __old friends__ be forgotten,
And never _____?
Should old friends be forgotten,
And days of long ago?

Chorus:
For days of long ago, _____,
For days of long ago
We'll take a cup of kindness yet,
For days of long ago.

And there's a hand, _____,
And give me a hand of yours,
And we'll take _____,
For days of long ago!

When you sing this song, you stand in a circle. For the first verse you hold hands with the people next to you. For the second verse you cross your arms and then hold hands.

Happy New Year

At midnight you say, 'A Guid New Year to ane an' a'!' ('A good New Year to one and all!'), or just, 'Happy New Year!'

First-footing

Immediately after midnight, people visit their neighbours' houses. But the first visitor must be a tall dark man (because fair-haired men are associated with Viking invaders!). This 'first-footer' brings gifts of a piece of coal, a small fruit cake (called a black bun), a bottle of whisky, and a silver coin. These represent warmth, food and drink, and money for the coming year.

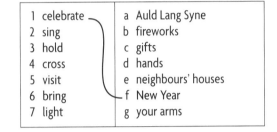

Edinburgh

In Edinburgh the celebrations begin a few days before Hogmanay. There is a procession on the night of 29th December. People pull a big model of a Viking warship right through the city. Then they light fireworks and burn the ship. On 30th December there is a pre-Hogmanay party in George Street, with a ceilidh* and pipe band parades. Then on New Year's Eve there is a huge street party for 200,000 people. It starts at 10 p.m. and goes on all night.

* /keɪliː/ – a party with Scottish dancing.

3 Answer the questions.
1 Where is the best place in Britain to celebrate New Year? _Scotland_
2 What is the language of the Scottish Highlands called?
3 What is the connection between the Scots and the Flemish?
4 What is the name of the song that people sing at New Year?
5 What is the song about?
6 What is a 'first footer'?
7 Why does a first footer bring a piece of coal into the house?
8 How long do the celebrations in Edinburgh last?

4a Match the verbs on the left with the phrases on the right.

1 celebrate	a Auld Lang Syne
2 sing	b fireworks
3 hold	c gifts
4 cross	d hands
5 visit	e neighbours' houses
6 bring	f New Year
7 light	g your arms

4b *On* or *at*?

| On 30th December ... | At 10 p.m. ... |
| On New Year's Eve ... | At midnight ... |

Write *on* or *at* to complete the sentences.
1 The ceilidh's .... Saturday. It starts ... 9 p.m.
2 It's my birthday .... 15th January. I usually have a party ... my birthday.
3 Everyone goes home .... lunchtime ... Christmas Eve.

What do you think?

▶ How do you feel about New Year's Eve?

I love New Year's Eve because we always have a big party.

I don't like New Year's Eve. I prefer Christmas because that's when you get presents.

New Year's Eve in Scotland sounds fun. I'd like to spend New Year's Eve in Edinburgh.

PROJECT

Write a short entry for a travel guide about New Year celebrations in one of the following countries. Use the Internet to help you.

Japan   Venezuela   Italy   Australia

7

CULTURE
Pantomime

1 Answer the questions.
  1 What classic films and TV programmes are on TV at Christmas?
  2 What's usually on at the cinema at Christmas?
  3 What's usually on at the theatre?

2 Read the text about pantomime.

Most cities and towns in the UK put on a pantomime at Christmas time. The most popular pantomimes are comedy versions of traditional children's stories, such as *Cinderella*, *Aladdin*, *Snow White* and *Jack and the Beanstalk*. It's the classic family entertainment at this time of year and it's often a child's first experience of theatre. The pantomime season is short. It runs from the middle of December until after New Year.

Pantomimes have a strong story line in which good fights against bad. But good always wins in the end. Typical characters include:

❖ the pantomime Dame (an older woman)
❖ the Principal Boy
❖ a 'good' character
❖ a 'bad' character
❖ a pantomime horse or cow.

A man plays the part of the Dame. A girl plays the Principal Boy. Two actors play the pantomime horse or cow – one plays the front half and the other plays the back half. (Yes, it's completely crazy!)

There is always audience participation. The children especially love to join in, and they boo and hiss when a bad character comes on stage. They warn the good characters when the villain is near (they shout, 'He's behind you!'). And they argue with the Dame or with other comic characters.

Let's take the example of *Cinderella*. The Dame – played by a man, remember – is Cinderella's stepmother. She makes Cinderella do all the housework while her own daughters, the Ugly Sisters, do nothing. The Principal Boy – played by a woman, remember – is Prince Charming, who falls in love with Cinderella. Men always play the part of the Ugly Sisters. They are the main comic characters, and the audience loves to argue with them. One of the Ugly Sisters says something like: 'I'm much more beautiful than Cinderella.' The audience shouts: 'Oh no you're not!' The Ugly Sister shouts back: 'Oh yes I am!' The audience shouts back: 'Oh no you're not!' And so it goes on.

There are always songs and jokes in pantomimes. While the stories are traditional, the songs can be pop songs with new words, and the jokes are topical and often better understood by the adults in the audience. Slapstick humour (comic acting where the actors hit each other, fall over, etc.) is an important part of pantomime. For example, the Ugly Sisters push each other to get to the Prince; pantomime horses and cows push and kick people to make them fall over.

Television personalities, comedians, actors and pop stars often appear in pantomimes, as this brings in big audiences and makes everything funnier. Everyone enjoys seeing a celebrity do something silly!

3 Complete the chart.

Pantomime

1 Where?	In *theatres* in most towns and cities in the .
2 When?	At
3 For how long?	From the middle of until .
4 Examples of pantomime stories	
5 Typical characters	
6 Details of characters: the Dame the Principal Boy the pantomime horse / cow	The Dame is a dressed as a . The Principal Boy is a dressed as a . There are actors inside the pantomime horse / cow.
7 Features of pantomime:	• traditional … • songs and topical … • participation • humour • good and _____ characters • celebrities such as …

4 Find the words in the text for:
1 most important *principal*
2 a group of people who watch a play
3 not just watching, but doing something
4 to make a noise to show you don't like something
5 to make an angry noise like a snake
6 to tell someone of a danger before it happens
7 a bad person in a story
8 to say something very loud
9 to disagree with someone, often in an angry way
10 not someone's real mother
11 about something in the news at the moment
12 to hit something with your foot

5 Find the following phrasal verbs in the text and say what they mean in your language:
1 put on (a pantomime)
2 join in
3 shout back
4 go on
5 fall over

What do you think?

▶ Does the idea of pantomime appeal to you? Why? / Why not?
▶ Why do you think pantomime is popular with children?
▶ Where else do you find slapstick?

PROJECT

Write the plot of Cinderella as a short story to read to an English child. Use these words and phrases to help you:

invitation	midnight
ball	lose (a shoe)
accept	try on (the shoe)
fairy godmother	(the shoe) fits / doesn't fit
pumpkin	marry
coach	

Start like this:
Cinderella lives with her father, stepmother and two stepsisters (the Ugly Sisters).
Prince Charming sends them an invitation to a ball at the palace. The Ugly Sisters accept the invitation but Cinderella's stepmother tells her she can't go. …
Practise reading the stories aloud to each other in class.

8

CULTURE

An English village

1 Answer the questions, and then read the text about Barrington.

1 When does a village become a small town? When the population is over 500? 1000? 2000?

2 What are the advantages and disadvantages of living in a village for
   a) children?   b) teenagers?   c) families?   d) old people?

Many village names in Britain end in –*ton*. 'Ton' means 'farm' in Old English.

Barrington, near Cambridge, is a traditional English village. It is over a thousand years old. Today, it has 920 inhabitants. The centre of the village is the village green, an open, grassy area for sports and recreation. At weekends in summer there is often a cricket match on the green and in winter the village football club plays there. Most village greens are quite small. Barrington has the longest village green in England.

In Barrington there are thatched cottages around the green. They are more than two hundred years old. The walls of the oldest cottages are made of wood and earth. Straw or reeds are used for the thatched roofs. The village pub, The Royal Oak, is on the edge of the green, almost opposite the duck pond. It is the oldest thatched pub in England. The twelfth-century All Saints Church is at the other end of the green.

The village hall is near the pub. It's a meeting place for village clubs. It's also a place where villagers can have parties.

The shop in the centre of the village sells basic items for the home (such as washing-up liquid, washing powder and toilet paper); it also sells food and newspapers. It's open seven days a week. There's a post office in the shop and a post box in front of the shop, where you can post letters.

There is a school in the village for children aged 5–11. The older children go by bus to a secondary school in a bigger village nearby. The oldest part of the primary school dates from 1838. Many village primary schools in England date from around that time. The primary school is next to the church and opposite the church there is a children's playground.

Most of the people who live in Barrington are not originally from the village. They're from towns and cities and they live in Barrington because they want a nice, quiet country life.

2 What are the places shown on the map? Read the text and label them.

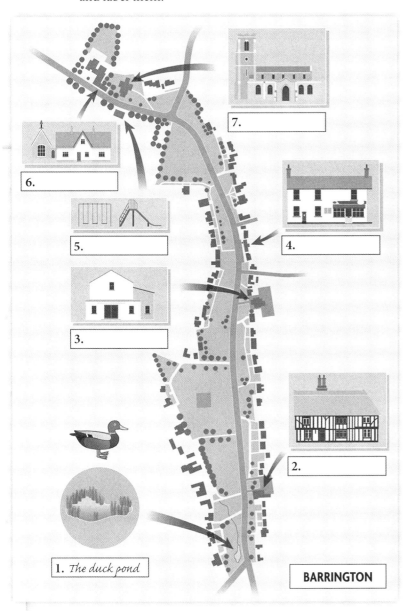

1. The duck pond
2.
3.
4.
5.
6.
7.

BARRINGTON

3 Answer the questions.
1. How many people live in Barrington? _920_
2. What is a village green?
3. When do people usually play cricket?
4. What's special about Barrington village green?
5. What's the word for a small old house?
6. What is a thatched cottage?
7. What is The Royal Oak?
8. How old is the church?
9. What do people use the village hall for?
10. What can you buy at the shop?
11. What do you call a school for children aged 5–11?
12. Why do people choose to live in Barrington?

4 Label the pictures with the prepositions / prepositional phrases in the box.

- in • in front of • in the centre of • ~~near~~
- next to • on • ~~on the edge of~~ • opposite

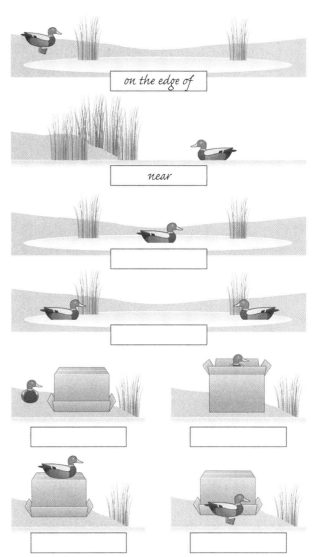

What do you think?

▶ What are the similarities and differences between a typical village in your country and a typical English village?
▶ Is 'village life' under threat nowadays? If so, why?
▶ Would you like to live in Barrington? Give your reasons.

PROJECT

Find out about a typical village in your country. Write a description of it for a tourist guide for foreign visitors, similar to the description of Barrington.

9

CULTURE

Two schools in India and Pakistan

1 Why do many people in India and Pakistan speak English? Read the text and check.

India became part of the British Empire in 1858 and gained independence on 15th August, 1947. A new country, Pakistan, was also born on that day. Until 1947 they were one nation fighting together to end British rule.

Today, India is the third largest country of English speakers after the USA and the UK. English is the second official language, but the main language of government. Two hundred million Indians use English fairly regularly. And for forty million people who use English as their main language, it is an essential sign of being 'educated'.

Seventeen million Pakistanis use English. It is the official language of government.

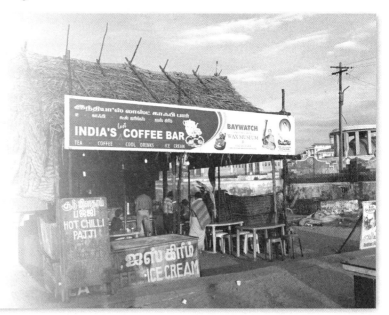

2 Read about primary and secondary education in India and Pakistan.

INDIA

The school year begins in April in most of the north and east, and in June in most of the south and west.

90% of boys and 84% of girls enrol at primary school. More boys than girls go on to secondary school.

73% of Indian men and 48% of Indian women can read.

PAKISTAN

The school year runs from September to June with a three-month summer holiday. However, in the north of the country, schools close for two months in winter because of heavy snow, so they have a shorter summer holiday.

76% of boys and 56% of girls enrol at primary school. More boys than girls go on to secondary school.

63% of men and 36% of women can read.

3 Are the sentences true or false?
1 Pakistan didn't exist before 1947. _True_
2 After 1947, India and Pakistan were part of the British Empire.
3 The school year is the same in India and Pakistan.
4 There are more boys than girls at primary school in India and Pakistan.
5 In both countries, the percentage of children at secondary school is the same as at primary school.
6 Literacy is higher in India than in Pakistan.

4 Work with a partner.

Student A: Read the information about Kendriya Vidyalaya Number 2 School on p21 and make notes in answer to the questions.

Student B: Read the information about Crescent Model School on p21 and make notes in answer to the questions.
1 Where is the school and what is special about it?
2 Is the school for both boys and girls?
3 Lessons are in English and which other language?
4 Can you choose which language you want to learn History and Geography in? What about Maths and Science?
5 What sort of sports and activities can you do outside lessons?

KENDRIYA VIDYALAYA NUMBER 2 SCHOOL, DELHI, INDIA

There are nearly a thousand Kendriya Vidyalaya schools in India. Number 2 School in Dehli, with over 5,000 students, is the largest of them. There are so many students that the school has two 'shifts': students choose to go to the first shift in the morning or the second in the afternoon.

The school is co-educational, that is, it's for boys and girls. It emphasises equality and secular education. Lessons are in Hindi or English and you can choose which language you want to learn in.

Extra-curricular activities are a vital part of the students' lives. The day begins with yoga and singing. The school believes that this is the best way to prepare students for lessons. After school, students play sports like basketball, volleyball, football and hockey. They also play 'Kho kho', which is like a game of 'tag': the object of the game is to tag (touch) members of the opposing team. Arts and crafts, and music and dance are as important as regular school subjects. There is even a 'Youth Parliament', to give the students the opportunity to develop their debating skills.

CRESCENT MODEL SCHOOL, LAHORE, PAKISTAN

Crescent Model School is in the heart of the Pakistani city of Lahore.

The school is co-educational but there are two separate campuses, one for boys and one for girls. There are about 4,600 students in total, of whom 1,500 are girls.

The school follows the Lahore Board curriculum but also runs classes for pupils who are interested in taking British exams such as A levels.

Students speak Urdu at home and it's also a subject on the school timetable. The medium of instruction in the school for all other subjects is English, but students can choose to learn History, Geography and Islamic Studies in Urdu. The school also conducts debates and poetry competitions in which students can choose between English and Urdu.

Crescent Model School has good sports facilities, including a swimming pool.

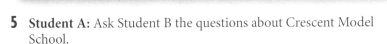

5 **Student A:** Ask Student B the questions about Crescent Model School.

Student B: Ask Student A the questions about Kendriya Vidyalaya School.

6 Make a list of the extra-curricular activities mentioned in the texts. What extra-curricular activities do schools in your country do?

What do you think?

▸ Do you think it's a good idea to have lessons in a language other than your mother tongue? What are the advantages and disadvantages?

▸ What are the advantages and disadvantages of co-educational schools?

PROJECT

Write a profile of your school for a promotional brochure.

... School is (in the heart of the city / in an area called ...

The school is (co-educational / a girls' school / a boys' school).

There are about ... students, (... boys and ... girls).

When students are ... years old, they take (the ... exam / exams in ...)

All students have lessons in Maths, ... You can also choose to do ... .

Extra-curricular activities include ... .

You can also play ... .

10 CULTURE
February Festivals

1 Answer the questions.
1. Do you celebrate any festivals in February? What are they?
2. Do people in your country do anything special for Lent, the period before Easter?

2 Read the texts.

Shrove Tuesday, Ash Wednesday and Lent

Shrove Tuesday (or Pancake Day in the UK) is the traditional feast day before the start of Lent on Ash Wednesday. Lent, the forty days before Easter, was a time of fasting for most people in the past. Shrove Tuesday was the last opportunity to have a good meal before Lent and eat up all the food which you couldn't eat during Lent (mostly food from animals, e.g. meat, eggs, and milk). One way of using up eggs and milk is to mix them with flour and cook them in butter. And that's how the tradition of eating pancakes on Shrove Tuesday began. (Pancakes were also seen as a symbol of the returning sun: round, gold and warm.)

Ash Wednesday is the day after Shrove Tuesday. It's called Ash Wednesday because ash, (what is left after a fire) symbolises the death of an old life. It's the first day of Lent, when traditionally people reflect on their old lives and think about living a better life.

It's a time to give up life's luxuries. Even today, people who aren't religious give up something for Lent, such as chocolate, sweets, cigarettes or alcohol.

Nowadays, families in the UK still eat pancakes on Shrove Tuesday. They eat them with lemon juice and sugar. People also take part in pancake races. They try to run with a pancake in a frying pan. They have to toss the pancake at least three times as they run.

Valentine's Day

VALENTINE'S DAY is on 14th February. Its origins are in the Roman festival of Lupercalia. During the festival, it was a popular custom to put pieces of paper with young girls' names on them into a box. The young men took one of the names from the box, and the two were then partners for the time of the celebrations.

Valentine's Day is celebrated mainly in English-speaking countries. The most popular custom is to send a card with a message to the person you love. The first Valentine message was from a priest called Valentine. It was at the time of the cruel Roman Emperor Claudius II. For Claudius, married men were not good soldiers because they were unhappy when they were away from their wives, so it wasn't possible to get married when he was emperor. Valentine was put in prison for helping lovers to marry in secret. The first 'Valentine messages' were from Valentine to his jailer's daughter, with whom he was in love. Christians in later years wanted to give the festival of Lupercalia a Christian connection, so they made Valentine a saint and named the festival after him.

The first Valentine message in the form of a poem was from the Duke of Orleans to his wife in 1415, when the Duke was in prison in the Tower of London.

Over 1 billion Valentine cards are sent in the US every year. Today people send flowers and chocolates as well as cards. Sometimes people make up poems to write in the card. The poems are often a variation on the lines:

> Roses are red
> Violets are blue
> Sugar is sweet
> And so are you.

The cards are decorated with flowers, hearts and a cupid (reflecting the Roman origins of Valentine's Day). The message in the card is 'Be my Valentine!' or 'From your Valentine – guess who?!'

3 Match the words (1–10) with the definitions (a–j).

1 feast	b	6 toss	
2 fasting		7 custom	
3 reflect on		8 prison	
4 death		9 jailer	
5 luxuries		10 cupid	

a a place to keep criminals
b a big meal for a special occasion
c think about carefully
d not eating any food
e something you usually do, a traditional activity
f the end of life
g the guard at a prison
h the Roman god of love
i things that are expensive and that you don't really need
j throw up in the air

4 Read the first text and answer these questions.
1 What is the other name for Shrove Tuesday?
2 What's the name of the period before Easter?
3 When is Ash Wednesday?
4 Why is it called Ash Wednesday?
5 People in the UK still keep traditions connected with Shrove Tuesday and Lent. Give two examples.

5 Write the questions for these answers.
1 It's on 14th February.
2 It was a Roman festival in February.
3 He was a priest in Roman times.
4 He was in prison for helping people to marry.
5 You send a card with a message to the person you love.

6 Find these phrasal verbs in the texts. Then use them to complete the sentences.

eat up	(= eat until there is nothing left)
use up	(= use completely)
give up	(= stop doing)
make up	(= invent)

1 A good writer can _____ a story about anything.
2 _____ your vegetables, they're good for you.
3 My dad wants to _____ smoking, so he's trying hypnotism.
4 Don't _____ all the hot water. I want a shower too!

What do you think?

▶ Put the opinions about celebrating festivals into the correct column.

Most people aren't religious any more so there's no point.

It keeps you in touch with the past.

We all need to have fun now and again.

Some festivals are just an excuse for shops to make money.

Traditions are an important part of your culture.

You don't need to have Pancake Day now because nobody fasts for Lent.

For	Against

Which of the opinions do you agree with?

PROJECT

Make a Valentine card using your own four-line Valentine's poem, and a short message. Start with: *Roses are red / Violets are blue ...*

Roses are red
Violets are blue
I'm your Valentine
Can you guess who?

Roses are red
Violets are blue
Frankenstein's monster
Looks just like you.

Tip: you can use one of the following words to rhyme with 'blue': *do, new, Peru, queue, shampoo, shoe, tattoo, too, true, two, who, you, zoo*

11

CULTURE

A nice cup of tea

1 Answer the questions.
1. When do you drink tea? (In the morning, in the afternoon, when you are ill ...)
2. What sort of tea do people in your country drink? (Black tea, green tea, herbal tea ...) How do they drink it? (With sugar, milk, lemon ...)

2 Read about tea in Britain.

3 True or false?
1. It's a British custom to offer tea in a crisis. *True*
2. Tea is popular with young people.
3. British people drink more tea than Turkish people.
4. If someone wants to reassure a friend that a situation is not as bad as it seems, they can say, "Don't worry. It's a storm in a teacup."
5. Most British people make tea in a teapot, with loose-leaf tea.
6. You can't make a really good cup of tea quickly.
7. You have to boil the water for three minutes.
8. Most British people have a cup of tea in the morning and another in the afternoon.

Tea in Britain

When you visit most people in Britain, the first thing they will do is put the kettle on and offer you some tea. For British people over a certain age, a cup of tea is the traditional answer to any of life's problems ...

A What's the matter, dear? You look awful!

B I lost my job yesterday, and the cat died this morning.

A I'll put the kettle on. You'll feel much better after a nice cup of tea.

Although coffee is the preferred drink of young people nowadays, Britons are still the world's second biggest tea drinkers (the Turks are number one). Tea appears in many popular expressions ...

'It's not my cup of tea.' (= I don't like it.)

'It's a storm in a teacup.' (= It's a lot of fuss about nothing.)

'I wouldn't go there, not for all the tea in China.' (= I would *never* go there.)

Tea is also an indicator of social class. Only a middle-/upper-class minority make tea with loose leaf tea. They drink it at breakfast, and mid-afternoon.

How to make the perfect cup of tea

- You must use loose leaf tea.
- You must warm the teapot.
- Put in one teaspoon of tea per person, plus one 'for the pot'.
- The water must be boiling when you pour it into the teapot.
- Allow the tea to stand for three minutes before you pour it into cups.
- Add cold milk and sugar to taste.

Most people use tea bags, and they drink tea throughout the day.

How to make a quick cup of tea

- Put the tea bag in a mug.
- Pour on hot water.
- Stir with a spoon.
- Take the tea bag out.
- Add milk (and sugar).

4 Read this article about the history of tea in Europe.

It was Dutch traders, at the end of the sixteenth century, who first brought tea to Europe. The first tea came from China to Holland via the island of Java, where the Dutch had a trading post. Tea soon became a fashionable drink in Holland. From there it spread to continental western Europe. But it was very expensive so it was only a drink for the wealthy.

The first reference to tea in Britain is from an advert in a newspaper from September, 1658. It announced that the 'China Drink, called by the Chinese *Tcha*, by other nations *Tay*, alias *Tee*', was on sale at a coffee house in the city of London.

The British took to tea drinking with great enthusiasm, but it was very expensive because there were high taxes on it. This provided an opportunity for smugglers and an illegal trade in cheap tea, which helped to make tea drinking more popular with ordinary people. Smuggling became such a problem that in 1785 the government decided to cut the tax on tea from 119% to 12.5%. The smuggling of tea stopped almost overnight.

British colonists in India started growing tea first in Assam and then in other regions. By 1888 Britain imported more tea from India than from China.

Just two days after the Second World War started, the British Government took control of all tea stocks. They moved all the tea from the warehouses in London to other parts of the country, because of the risk of bombing. The British wartime Prime Minister, Winston Churchill, said, 'Tea is more important to soldiers than munitions.' Britain needed its tea!

5 Complete the timeline.

Late 1500s _____

1658 _____

Tea became very popular in Britain. Smugglers brought tea into Britain illegally.

1785 _____

By 1888 _____

1939 _____

6 Find the words in the text for these people:
1 people who buy and sell things *traders*
2 people who have a lot of money
3 people who bring things into a country illegally
4 people who take over another country and go to live there
5 the head of the government
6 people in the army

What do you think?

▸ How do tea-drinking habits in your country compare with those in Britain?
In my country, most people drink coffee at breakfast time. They drink tea ... .
Young people ... .

▸ Why do you think tea and coffee are so popular?

PROJECT

Find out about the history of coffee in Europe. Design a timeline, like the one in Exercise 5, for a wallchart. You could include some illustrations.

1615	Venetian traders brought coffee to Italy from the East.
	Christian priests said that coffee (which came from the Muslim world) was the drink of Satan. The pope, however, disagreed and blessed coffee as a Christian drink.
1650	The first coffee house in Europe opened in Oxford.

12

CULTURE

A walk through London

1 Match the descriptions to the places on the map.

   a It's a big clock.   b The royal family live here.   c It's a famous department store. It sells everything.
   d You can see Shakespeare's plays here.   e It's a big art gallery.   f The British government meets here.

2 Read and check your answers to Exercise 1.

A walk through London
(2 hours)

❼ St Paul's Cathedral
There was once a Roman temple of the goddess Diana in the place where St Paul's Cathedral now stands. The present cathedral is the fifth one on this site. Sir Christopher Wren designed and built it after the Great Fire of London in 1666. Make sure you go to the Whispering Gallery, 30 metres above the floor. If you whisper next to the wall, someone can you hear you on the opposite side of the gallery, 33 metres away.

❷ Buckingham Palace
The Queen lives here when she is in London. The palace has six hundred rooms, a swimming pool and a cinema. The Queen has a suite of 12 rooms on the first floor. Every year she has three garden parties and there are eight thousand people at each one. To celebrate 50 years of her reign, there was a pop concert and firework display in the garden.

❹ The Thames
The Romans came to Britain nearly two thousand years ago. They started to build a city, which they called 'Londinium', next to the 'Tamesis', the river Thames.

❶ Harrods
In 1849 Henry Charles Harrod bought a small shop in the village of Knightsbridge. He sold food and everyday items. An advertisement in *The Daily Telegraph* in 1894 said: "Harrods serves the world." In 1898 it had the first escalator in London. An assistant stood at the top of the escalator with smelling salts and brandy for nervous customers. Now Harrods is one of the world's largest department stores.

❸ Big Ben and the Houses of Parliament
Big Ben is the most famous clock in Britain. It's at the top of St Stephen's Tower, next to the Houses of Parliament. The Houses of Parliament, also known as the Palace of Westminster, are the home of the British Government.

Headway Culture and Literature Companion Elementary

8 The Tower of London
When William of Normandy conquered Britain and became King William I in 1066, he built the Tower of London to show his power. In the early years, the Tower was both a prison and a royal palace. One of the prison cells was just over one metre square, so a prisoner could not stand or lie down. In the thirteenth century, King Henry III kept lions, leopards and an elephant there. In 1252 the king of Norway gave Henry a polar bear. The bear was on a chain so that it could go and catch fish in the river. At that time, the public could go to see the animals – the price was $1\frac{1}{2}$ pence but it was free if you took a cat or dog to feed to the lions! Today, you can visit the Tower to see the crown jewels.

6 The Globe Theatre
Going to the theatre was very popular in Shakespeare's time. It wasn't just for rich people. At the Globe Theatre you paid just one penny to stand. Shakespeare appeared in his own plays at the Globe. But the original theatre burnt down during a performance of one of his plays when the actors fired a cannon and set fire to the thatched roof! The new Globe Theatre is a copy of the original one.

5 Tate Modern
If you like modern painting and sculpture, this is the place for you. It's free to go in and the building itself is well worth seeing – it's actually an old power station. The views over the Thames are fantastic.

3 Read the text again and answer the questions.
Who
1 Who called the Thames 'Tamesis'? *The Romans.*
2 Who was the architect of St Paul's Cathedral?
What
3 What was the Roman name for London?
4 What happened to the original Globe Theatre?
5 What kind of event does the Queen regularly have at Buckingham Palace?
Where
6 Where did William I come from?
7 Where can you go if you like art?
8 Where do British politicians discuss important questions?
9 Where was the first escalator in London?
When
10 When was the Tower of London a zoo?
11 When was the Great Fire of London?
Why
12 Why did William I build the Tower of London?
13 Why do people go to the Tower of London today?
How
14 How did Harrods help customers who were nervous about using the escalator?

4 Guess the meaning of the following words from their contexts:
1 reign   3 burnt down   5 chain
2 display   4 whisper   6 conquered

5 Write down an example of each of the following (it can be anywhere in the world). Compare lists with your partner. How many of the places on your list does your partner know?

| a tower | a cathedral | a prison | a gallery |
| a palace | a theatre | a temple | a department store |

What do you think?

▸ You're spending the day in London. You can only go to two places. Which would you choose and why?

I'd go to Harrods first because it's famous and I love shopping.

Yes, but you can go to department stores any time. I'd go to the Tower of London. I'd love to see the crown jewels.

▸ Which two places would you recommend people to see in your city?

I'd tell them to go to (...) because (...).

No, I don't agree. I'd tell them to go to (...) because (...).

PROJECT

Plan a two-hour walk through your home town or city for a tourist guide. Write brief descriptions of the interesting places to see and illustrate your plan.

13

CULTURE

Robin Hood – England's most famous folk hero

1 Answer the questions.
   1 Which of these folk heroes do you know? What do you know about them? Which of them are real people?

   Zorro, William Tell, Til Eulenspiegel, El Cid, Ned Kelly, Joan of Arc, The Little Dutch Boy

   2 What is a folk hero? Are folk heroes necessarily real people?

2 Read the text about Robin Hood.

(1) _____

Stories describing the adventures of Robin Hood have been popular for over six hundred years. They tell of a brave young man who robbed the rich to give to the poor.

(2) _____

Legal records from 1226 mention an outlaw called 'Robert Hod'. In 1262 royal records mention an outlaw called William de Fevre, who had the nickname William Robehood, or Robinhood. By 1300 there were at least five other outlaws who had the nickname Robin Hood. Was there one real Robin Hood? We don't know.

(3) _____

Life in Britain was hard. Most people were poor peasants but they paid very high taxes. The law did not protect them. ('Sheriffs', responsible for enforcing the law, were not necessarily interested in justice for the poor.) Robin Hood was an 'outlaw' because he lived outside the law. He and his band of men (and women) helped ordinary people. They lived in Sherwood Forest, near Nottingham. The forest covered a large area of about 100,000 acres. It was the perfect place for Robin and the others to live and hide from their main enemies, Prince John and the Sheriff of Nottingham.

(4) _____

Robin's band of men included Little John, Friar Tuck and Allan-a-Dale. Little John's name was ironic, because he wasn't at all small – he was tall and very strong. Friar Tuck was a monk who loved beer, food and a good time. He was happy and cheerful. He looked slow but he was quick-witted. Allan-a-Dale was a loyal servant to Robin. He was also a musician who wrote and sang ballads of Robin's adventures. They were all good archers but Robin's skill with the bow and arrow was second to none.

(5) _____

There's one important woman in the later, more romantic stories. Her parents were dead and, in some versions of the story, she was Prince John's niece. Her name was Maid Marian and Robin was in love with her. She became Robin's wife.

3 Choose a heading for each paragraph of the text.

Life in the thirteenth century
How old is the story of Robin Hood? _1_
Robin's true love
The outlaws
Fact or fiction?

4 Complete the story using the information from the text on p28.

The story of Robin Hood

KING Richard I went to fight in the Crusades and left his brother, Prince (1) __John__, in charge of the country. John was an evil man. Together with the (2) _____ of Nottingham, he raised (3) _____ so high that poor people could not pay them.

Robin Hood and his (4) _____ of men and women lived in Sherwood (5) _____, which is close to (6) _____. Prince John's men collected the taxes from the village people. But Robin and his men, who were all excellent archers, were always ready with their bows and (7) _____. They stopped the prince's men in the forest and took the money to give back to the (8) _____. The sheriff never managed to stop Robin and his men from giving back the taxes to the poor.

Prince John was angry and knew that Robin was in love with his (9) _____, Maid Marian. He organised an archery contest to trap Robin. The prize was marriage to Marian. Robin was a good (10) _____ but he knew it was dangerous to take part, so he went in disguise and he won. However, Prince John realised who he was. He arrested Robin and imprisoned him in Nottingham Castle. Marian helped Robin's men to free him from prison and then went to live in Sherwood Forest, where she and Robin were married.

Statue of Robin and Marian in Edwinstowe village

5 Try to guess the meaning of the following words from their contexts:

1 legal records
2 nickname
3 peasants
4 taxes
5 hide from
6 ironic
7 archer
8 second to none
9 trap
10 in disguise

6 Find these adjectives in the text. Which of them describe a typical folk hero?

brave	evil	ordinary	young	happy
quick-witted	dangerous	slow	poor	
tall	cheerful	angry	strong	loyal

Are there any adjectives you would add?
(young? good-looking? ...)

What do you think?

▶ Why do you think Robin Hood was and still is a popular folk hero? Do you think there was a real person like him?

PROJECT

Write about a folk hero of your choice, for a website called 'Folk heroes from around the world'. Think about the following:
• Is he / she real or fictional (or both)?
• Where and when did he / she live?
• What was life like then?
• Why is he / she a folk hero?

14 CULTURE
New Zealand

1. How many questions about New Zealand can you answer before you read the text?
   1. Where is New Zealand?
   2. Approximately how many people live in New Zealand?
   3. What's the capital city called?
   4. Which languages do New Zealanders speak?
   5. What's the climate like?
   6. Can you name some recent successful films made in New Zealand?
   7. Why do you think people want to make films there?
   8. What kind of sports can you do in New Zealand?
   9. What's the name of the New Zealand national rugby team?
   10. What is the 'haka'?
   11. What is a kiwi?
   12. What are the indigenous people of New Zealand called?
   13. Who was the first European to reach New Zealand?
   14. Which European nation first settled in New Zealand?

2. Read the text and check or complete your answers to Exercise 1.

NEW ZEALAND consists of two main islands, North Island and South Island, and several small islands, surrounded by the South Pacific Ocean. Both the main islands are mountainous. South Island has the Southern Alps running from top to bottom. It also has many glaciers and rivers. North Island is more heavily populated. As well as mountains, it has volcanoes, hissing geysers, boiling mud and hot springs. Both islands have forests, deep, clear lakes and long, deserted beaches. The main cities are Wellington, Auckland (both on the North Island) and Christchurch (South Island).

The vast areas of dramatic countryside have made New Zealand a perfect location for films such as *Lord of the Rings* and *Prince Caspian*. Its natural features also make New Zealand an ideal place for outdoor activities such as fishing, hiking, skiing, canoeing, kayaking, mountain biking, rock climbing, caving, windsurfing, white water rafting, kite boarding, paragliding, ski diving, and bungee jumping.

New Zealand is famous for its national rugby team, called the All Blacks because they wear black shirts and black shorts. The players perform a 'haka' before each game. It's an ancient Maori war dance and its purpose is to make the players feel strong and to 'psyche out' the opposing team.

The kiwi and the tuatara are two animal species that are only found in New Zealand. The kiwi is a small black bird which can't fly. (There were two airlines that started with the name 'Kiwi Airlines' in the 1990s. They both went bankrupt after a few years!) The tuatara is the most ancient of all living reptiles. It's 200 million years old – even older than the dinosaurs.

New Zealand people are called New Zealanders. They're nicknamed 'kiwis', like the bird, which is the country's unofficial symbol. New Zealanders are known for being easy-going, friendly and egalitarian. And New Zealand is one of the few countries where the police don't carry guns.

FACT FILE

Population	4 million
Capital City	Wellington
Currency	New Zealand dollar
Languages	English and Maori
Climate	Temperate, neither very hot nor very cold.

3 Match the words with their meanings:

1 glacier	7 reptile	
2 geyser	8 nicknamed	
3 mud	9 to claim	
4 deserted	10 settler	
5 to psyche out	11 Gold rush	
6 ancient	12 to revolt	

a a mixture of earth and water
b a river of ice
c to say that something is yours
d a person who goes to live in a new country
e a race to find gold
f to take (violent) action against authority
g a natural spring that sends hot water and steam into the air
h very old
i a type of animal, such as a snake or a lizard
j given a funny name
k without people
l to use psychology to make someone feel afraid

4 Choose one of the outdoor activities mentioned in the text and describe it. Ask the other members of the class to guess which one it is.

You go down a river in a boat. It can be dangerous ...

What do you think?

▸ Would you like to go to New Zealand? Why?

   I've seen the Lord of the Rings *films and I thought the scenery was great, so I'd like to go there.*

▸ What would you most like to see or do there?

PROJECT

What are the key dates in your country's history? Write a sentence about each one to make a wallchart. Use the section on 'New Zealand History' as a model.

The Netherlands
55 BC The Romans arrived.
1555   The Netherlands became part of the Spanish Empire.

New Zealand History

800 AD	The Maori (the indigenous people) lived in New Zealand from around this date.
1642	The Dutch explorer, Abel Tasman, reached New Zealand but the Maoris prevented him from landing.
1769	Captain Cook arrived in New Zealand and claimed it for Britain.
1830s	British settlers started to arrive.
1840	The Treaty of Waitangi: many Maori chiefs gave up their land in return for British citizenship.
1860	Gold rush in Otago, South Island.
1860-72	New Zealand wars. The Maoris revolted against the British taking their land.
1893	New Zealand became the first country to give women the vote.
1947	New Zealand became an independent country.

15 LITERATURE
Roger McGough – Mafia Cats

1 Most people don't read poetry. Why?

2 Read about a well-known British poet, Roger McGough.

> *"Poetry is something that should be entertaining and accessible."* Roger McGough
>
> Roger McGough (born November 9th 1937) is a well-known poet from Liverpool. After studying at Hull University, he became a teacher. He knew the Beatles and wrote some of the script for their film *Yellow Submarine*. In the 1960s he was in a band called the Scaffold. In 1967 he and two other writers from Liverpool published a collection of poems called *The Mersey Sound*. The poems were amusing and easy to understand. The book sold more than a million copies.

Why was *The Mersey Sound* collection so popular?

3 Read the following paragraph and answer the question.

> Roger McGough sometimes writes poems about cats. One of the most famous poets of the twentieth century, T S Eliot, also wrote some poems about cats (they were the basis of the hit musical *Cats*). An eighth-century Irish monk wrote a poem about his white cat, Pangur, comparing his own work on a manuscript with the cat's work catching mice. An eighteenth-century English poet, Christopher Smart, wrote a long poem in honour of his cat called *My Cat Jeffrey*.

Why do you think people often write poems about cats?

4 Before you read Roger McGough's poem, answer these questions:

1 What is the Mafia? Which country is most famous for its Mafia? Do you know any other names for the Mafia?
2 Which of these activities are the Mafia usually involved in?
   - protection rackets (making people pay to stop bad things happening to them)
   - making wine
   - gambling (putting money on a card game, horse race, etc. in order to win more money)
   - tax fiddles (finding ways not to pay tax to the government)
   - insurance scams (getting money from insurance companies for things that didn't really happen)
   - selling hats and suits
   - vice (illegal activities involving sex and drugs)
3 What do the Mafia do with their enemies?

MAFIA CATS

We're the Mafia cats
Bugsy, Franco and Toni
We're crazy for pizza
With hot pepperoni

5 We run all the rackets
From gambling to vice
On St Valentine's Day
We *massacre mice

We always wear shades
10 To show that we're meanies
Big hats and sharp suits
And drive Lamborghinis

We're the Mafia cats
Bugsy, Franco and Toni
15 Love Sicilian wine
And cheese macaroni

But we have a secret
(And if you dare tell
You'll end up with the kitten
20 At the bottom of the well

Or covered in concrete
And thrown into the deep
For this is one secret
You must really keep.)

25 We're the Cosa Nostra
Run the scams and the fiddles
*But at home we are
   Mopsy, Ginger and Tiddles.*

*This is a reference to the St Valentine's Day massacre on 14th February, 1929, when members of Al Capone's gang shot and killed seven members of the North Side Gang in Chicago.

Mopsy, Ginger, Tiddles

5 Match these words and phrases to their definitions:

1 massacre	a) a building material which is hard when dry
2 shades	b) a deep hole from which you get water
3 meanies	c) a baby cat
4 sharp (suits)	d) killing a lot of people
5 dare	e) result in
6 end up with	f) sunglasses (*informal*)
7 kitten	g) unkind people (*in child's language*)
8 well	h) very smart, fashionable, well-fitting
9 concrete	i) have the courage to do something

6 Answer the questions.

1 How many Italian references can you find in the poem?

2 Why are the last two lines in *italics*?

3 Look at line 5: *We run all the rackets*. This is an example of alliteration (a line containing words beginning with the same sound, in this case /r/). Can you find two more examples of alliteration?

4 What point does the poem make about cats?

7 Perform the poem in class …

- Decide on the kind of accent you want to use (British? American?)
- Choose some actions to accompany certain lines of the poem (e.g. 'We're crazy for pizza')

You can either perform the poem as a whole class, in chorus; or you can divide the class into seven groups, taking one verse each.

What do you think?

▸ Do you like poetry?
▸ What kind of poetry do you like the most?
▸ Do you think it's better if poetry has regular rhymes and rhythm?

Roger McGough thinks that the role of poetry is to make people feel better about themselves and the world, and to surprise them. He feels that poetry can change things.

In your view …
- why do people write poetry?
- why do people read poetry?
- can poetry 'change things'?

PROJECT

In Ancient Egypt the cat was sacred. In the Middle Ages people thought that the devil's favourite form was a black cat. What makes cats so different from other animals?

Write an email to an English friend who is trying to decide whether to get a cat or a dog, saying why you do or don't recommend a cat.

Cats are usually … (very independent / quiet / cruel / …)
In comparison, dogs …
Cats never …, but dogs …
Cats seem to … (be attracted to people who don't like cats)

16 LITERATURE

Mark Twain – *The Adventures of Tom Sawyer*

1. Do you know anything about Tom Sawyer?
2. Read about Mark Twain, the author of *The Adventures of Tom Sawyer*.

> **Mark Twain**
> 1835-1910
> Real name: Samuel Langhorne Clemens
> American writer, born in Florida, Missouri
> His most famous books are *The Adventures of Tom Sawyer* (1876) and *Huckleberry Finn* (1884). They are based on his own childhood experiences.

Do you know any other books in which children are the main characters?

3. Read extract A.

What do you learn about Tom and his Aunt Polly?

4a Look at the picture. Which boy is Tom? What is he doing, and why? Read extract B, and see if you were right.

Extract A

'Tom! *Tom!* Where are you?'
No answer.
'Where is that boy? When I find him, I'm going to ...'
5   Aunt Polly looked under the bed. Then she opened the door and looked out into the garden.
'*Tom!*'
She heard something behind her. A small boy ran past, but Aunt Polly put out her hand and stopped him.
10 'Ah, there you are! What's that on your hands? And your mouth?'
'I don't know, Aunt.'
'Well, I know. It's jam! My best jam!'
'Oh, Aunt Polly! Quick – look behind you!'
So Aunt Polly looked, and Tom was out of the house in a second.
15 She laughed quietly. 'I never learn. I love that Tom, my dead sister's child, but he isn't an easy boy for an old lady. Well, it's Saturday tomorrow and there's no school, but it isn't going to be a holiday for Tom. Oh no! He's going to work tomorrow.'

Extract B

Saturday was a beautiful day. It was summer and the sun was hot and there were flowers in all the gardens. It was a day for everybody to be happy.
Tom came out of his house with a brush and a big pot of white
5   paint in his hand. He looked at the fence; it was higher than him and thirty metres long. He put his brush in the paint and painted some of the fence. He did it again. Then he stopped and looked at the fence, put down his brush and sat down. There were hours of work in front of him and he was the unhappiest boy in the village.
10 After ten minutes Tom had an idea, a wonderful idea. He took up the brush again and began work. He saw Ben Rogers in the street, but he didn't look at him. Ben had an apple in his hand. He came up to Tom and looked at the fence.
'I *am* sorry, Tom.'
15 Tom said nothing. The paint brush moved up and down.
'Working for your aunt?' said Ben. 'I'm going down to the river. I'm sorry you can't come with me.'
Tom put down his brush. 'You call this work?' he said.
'Painting a fence?' said Ben. 'Of course it's work!'
20 'Perhaps it is and perhaps it isn't. But I like it,' said Tom. 'I can go to the river any day. I can't paint a fence very often.'
Ben watched Tom for about five minutes. Tom painted very slowly and carefully. He often stopped, moved back from the fence and looked at his work with a smile.

4b Answer the questions on extract B.
1. Why does the writer begin this part of the story with a description of the day?
2. How does Tom feel? Why?
3. When Ben sees Tom painting the fence, what does he think?
4. Why does Tom say, 'I can go to the river any day. I can't paint a fence very often'?
5. Why does Tom paint slowly and why does he smile?
6. What do you think Tom's 'wonderful idea' (l. 10) is?

5a Before you read extract C, say what you think is going to happen.

Extract C

Ben began to get very interested, and said:
'Tom, can I paint a little?'
Tom thought for a second. 'I'm sorry, Ben. You see, my aunt wants me to do it because I'm good at painting.
5 My brother Sid wanted to paint, too, but she said no.'
'Oh, please, Tom, just a little. I'm good at painting, too. Hey, do you want some of my apple?'
'No, Ben, I can't –'
'OK, you can have all my apple!'
10 Tom gave Ben the brush. He did not smile, but for the first time that day he was a very happy boy. He sat down and ate Ben's apple.
More friends came to laugh at Tom, but soon they all wanted to paint, too. By the afternoon Tom had three
15 balls, an old knife, a cat with one eye, an old blue bottle, and a lot of other exciting things. He was the richest boy in St Petersburg, and the fence – all thirty metres of it – was a beautiful white. He went back to the house.
'Aunt Polly! Can I go and play now?'
20 Aunt Polly came out of the house to look. When she saw the beautiful white fence, she was very pleased. She took Tom into the house and gave him an apple, telling him how much more people enjoy things when they've got them by being good and working hard.
25 'Well, you can go and play. But don't come home late.'
When Aunt Polly wasn't looking, Tom quickly took a doughnut and ran off.

5b Answer the questions.
1. Why doesn't Tom let Ben paint at first?
2. Why do other children come to see Tom painting the fence?
3. What was Tom's 'wonderful idea'?
4. Why was this a good day for everybody?

6 Look at the sentences containing a verb + preposition(s). How would you translate them into your language?

out of
Tom *came out of* his house. (B l. 4)

past
A small boy *ran past*. (A l. 8)

down
He *put down* his brush and *sat down*. (B l. 8)
I'm *going down* to the river. (B l. 16)

up
He *came up* to Tom. (B l. 12)

back
He *moved back* from the fence. (B l. 23)
He *went back* to the house. (C l. 18)

at
More friends came to *laugh at* Tom. (C l. 13)

off
He *ran off*. (C l. 27)

What do you think?

▶ Mark Twain was well-known for his humorous remarks, for example:

'It is good to obey all the rules when you're young, so you'll have the strength to break them when you're old.'

'A banker is a fellow who lends you his umbrella when the sun is shining, but wants it back the minute it begins to rain.'

'The first of April is the day we remember what we are the other 364 days of the year.'

What did he mean? Do you agree?

PROJECT

As a young man, Mark Twain worked as pilot on a steam boat and as a printer. He loved science and inventions.

Which of the following inventions appeared in Mark Twain's lifetime? Which of them are American inventions? Find out and write some key details about them for a website called 'The World of Mark Twain'.

- the steam boat
- the car
- the aeroplane
- photography
- cinematography
- the steam train
- the underground railway
- the telephone
- Morse code
- the radio

17

LITERATURE

Wendy Cope – Three poems

1 Read about the poet Wendy Cope.

Do you prefer to read poetry in silence, or to listen to someone reading it to you?

Most children like poems and respond well to them; most adults find poetry difficult and don't read it. Why?

> Wendy Cope was born in Kent in 1945. When she was a child, her parents often read poems to her. She worked as a primary school teacher in London before becoming a writer and critic. She has written several books of poetry and also two children's books. She visits schools to read her poems and to talk to the children.

2 Read these three poems by Wendy Cope.

The Orange

At lunchtime I bought a huge orange
The size of it made us all laugh.
I peeled it and shared it with Robert and Dave—
They got quarters and I had a half.

And that orange it made me so happy,
As ordinary things often do
Just lately. The shopping. A walk in the park
This is peace and contentment. It's new.

The rest of the day was quite easy.
I did all my jobs on my list
And enjoyed them and had some time over.
I love you. I'm glad I exist.

Valentine

My heart has made its mind up
And I'm afraid it's you.
Whatever you've got lined up,
My heart has made its mind up
And if you can't be signed up
This year, next year will do.
My heart has made its mind up
And I'm afraid it's you.

36 *Headway Culture and Literature Companion* Elementary

Kindness to animals

If I went vegetarian
And didn't eat lambs for dinner,
I think I'd be a better person
And also thinner.

But the lamb is not endangered
And at least I can truthfully say
I have never, ever eaten a barn owl,
So perhaps I am OK.

3 Answer the questions.

Orange

1 Is the emotion of this poem positive or negative? Which words (verbs, nouns, adjectives) contribute to this?
2 Why did Wendy Cope write the poem?
   a) To tell us how much she likes oranges.
   b) To describe the feeling of being in love.
   c) To give a picture of her everyday life.

Valentine

3 Match the expressions from the poem to the definitions.

1 to make your mind up	a to agree to be a member of a club
2 to have something lined up	b to decide
3 to be signed up	c to have something arranged, planned

4 What does 'I'm afraid' mean in the line 'I'm afraid it's you'?
   a) I'm frightened
   b) I'm sorry to say
   c) I'm certain
5 What does 'will do' mean in the line 'This year, next year will do'?
   a) will be OK
   b) will happen
   c) will be very busy
6 How does the poet feel in this poem? (Nervous, unsure, determined, jealous, depressed ...?)

Kindness to animals

7 What's the difference between 'a lamb/lambs' and 'lamb'? Which do you find on a menu? Why does the poet use 'lambs' in this poem?
8 Which of the following statements best describes the poet's attitude?
   a) She's seriously thinking of becoming vegetarian.
   b) She is very worried about eating meat, because it's not good for her.
   c) She's enjoying playing with the idea of being vegetarian, but it isn't for her.

What do you think?

"Poetry can help us to get in touch with our feelings. It can also make us laugh. It can help us celebrate how beautiful the world is."

"I think it's possible for a poem to be funny and serious at the same time."

Wendy Cope

▶ Do you agree with Wendy Cope? Can you find examples in the poems on these pages to support what she says?
▶ Which of the poems do you like, and why?
▶ How would you describe the kind of language she uses in her poems?

PROJECT

Learn one of the poems by heart ...
Oranges: Work in groups of three. Each person learns one verse.
Valentine: Work individually.
Kindness to animals: Work in pairs. Each person learns one verse.
Perform your poems to the class, or, if possible, to another class.

18 LITERATURE

Oscar Wilde – *The Canterville Ghost*

1 Read about Oscar Wilde.

2 *The Canterville Ghost* is a ghost story. Answer the questions and then read the extract.
  1 Why are ghost stories popular?
  2 What kind of buildings usually have ghosts?
  3 What do ghosts do to scare people?
  4 What do people do when they see a ghost?

> **OSCAR WILDE** was born in Dublin in 1854. He went to college there and then studied at Oxford University, where, in 1878, he won a poetry prize. In 1882 he went to the USA and stayed there for a year, travelling around the country and giving talks. In 1888 he wrote *The Happy Prince and Other Tales*, a book of stories for his sons.
>
> Oscar Wilde was a great storyteller. He wrote plays, poetry, short stories and a novel. *The Canterville Ghost*, a short story, was published in 1891.

The Canterville Ghost

AN AMERICAN BUSINESSMAN, Hiram B. Otis, buys a big old house in England from Lord Canterville. He comes to live there with his family: his wife, his eldest son Washington, his fifteen-year-old daughter Virginia, and his twin sons. The house is called Canterville Chase and it has a ghost, the Canterville Ghost. Mr Otis and his family are not afraid of the ghost because they come from America, a 'modern' country. Soon after their arrival, the ghost tries to frighten them but he doesn't succeed. So he tries again ...

On Sunday night, soon after the family went to bed, the ghost made his next move. There was a three-hundred-year-old suit of armour downstairs. 'Now, a ghost in armour will surely frighten even modern Americans,' he thought. He began to put on the suit of armour, but it was too heavy for him, and he and some of the armour fell to the floor with a loud CRASH.

All the men in the Otis family jumped out of bed and hurried downstairs at once.

They found the unhappy ghost sitting there, holding his head and crying softly with pain. The twins had their pea-shooters with them and immediately began to shoot little balls of paper at him. Mr Otis brought out his handgun and, like the good Californian he was, called out to the ghost:

'Hold up your hands!'

At this, the ghost jumped up with a wild and angry scream and flew through them. Washington Otis's candle went out and suddenly everything was dark. At the top of the stairs, the ghost turned to give his terrible ghostly laugh – the famous laugh which once turned Lord Raker's hair white in a single night. It went on and on until the house was full of sound.

A bedroom door opened and Mrs Otis appeared with a bottle in her hand. 'I'm afraid you're not feeling very well.' she said to the ghost. 'I've brought you some of Dr Dobell's special stomach medicine. If you're having trouble with your stomach, this will soon help you to feel better.'

The ghost looked at her angrily, and began to turn himself into a big black dog (one of his most famous tricks). But the sound of young footsteps coming up the stairs stopped him, and he quickly disappeared with a ghostly 'Oooooooh!' before the twins arrived at the top.

For some time after this he was very ill. But when he began to feel better, he decided to try for the third time to frighten Hiram B. Otis and his family.

He spent most of Friday, the 17th of August, trying to decide what to wear. At last he decided on a dead man's shroud, a large black hat with a red feather in it, and a long knife.

That night the wind shook all the doors and windows, and the rain crashed down on to the roof of the house. The ghost made his plans carefully.

3a Put the pictures in the correct order.

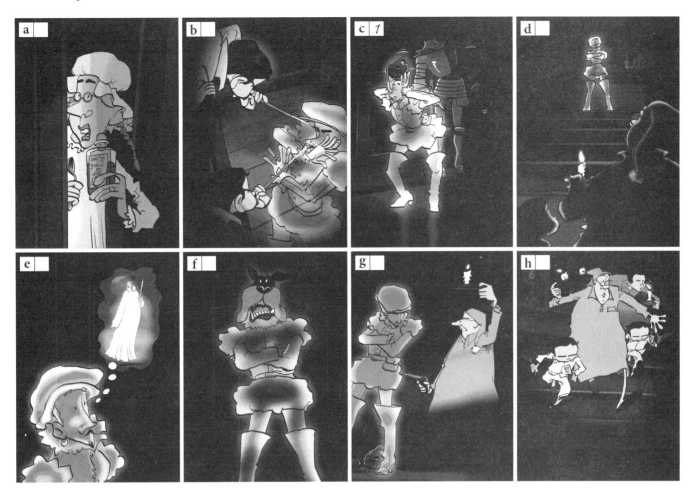

3b Find these things in the pictures:
- a suit of armour
- pea shooters
- a handgun
- a candle
- a bottle of medicine
- a feather
- a shroud

3c Write a short caption for each picture.
1 *The suit of armour was too heavy for the ghost.*

4a Complete the sentences with the words in the box. Then check your answers by looking back at the text.

| into | on (x3) | to | out (x3) | up (x2) | at |

1 The family went _____ bed.
2 The ghost began to put _____ the suit of armour.
3 The twins began to shoot balls of paper _____ the ghost.
4 Mr Otis brought _____ his handgun.
5 Mr Otis called _____ to the ghost.
6 Hold _____ your hands!
7 The ghost jumped _____ with a wild and angry scream.
8 Washington Otis's candle went _____ .
9 The ghost's terrible laugh went _____ and _____ .
10 The ghost began to turn himself _____ a big black dog.

4b How do you say each of the sentences in Exercise 4a in your language?

What do you think?

▸ What is unusual about this ghost story?
▸ Why does Oscar Wilde make the family American rather than British?
▸ Do you believe in ghosts?
▸ Why are ghosts usually unhappy in ghost stories?

PROJECT

'The ghost made his plans carefully.' What do you think the ghost does next?

Write the next episode in the story, reusing language from the text where you can. You can write three paragraphs, beginning:

At midnight, the ghost went to Washington Otis's room. He opened the door ...
Then he went to Mr Hiram B. Otis's room.
Finally, he went to the twins' room. But they had a surprise for him.

Read your stories aloud to each other.

19 LITERATURE

John Cooper Clarke – *I wanna be yours*

1 Read about John Cooper Clarke.

JOHN COOPER CLARKE (born January 25th 1949) is an English performance poet. He's from Salford, in the north of England. He became well-known during the 1970s – the time of punk rock – so he is sometimes called a punk poet. He appeared as an opening act for bands and singers such as the Sex Pistols, The Fall and Elvis Costello. He often introduces himself as 'Johnny Clarke – the name behind the hairstyle.'

What do you think 'punk poet' means?

Do you think a punk poet writes romantic poems?

2 Match these things to the pictures.
1. coffee pot
2. dreamboat
3. electric heater
4. electric meter
5. Ford Cortina
6. raincoat
7. ocean
8. setting lotion
9. teddy bear
10. vacuum cleaner

3 Which of these is a romantic thing to say?
1. I want to be your ...
   a) Valentine
   b) raincoat
   c) lover
   d) vacuum cleaner
   e) teddy bear
   f) electric heater

4 Read the poem.

I *wanna be yours ...

I wanna be your vacuum cleaner
breathing in your dust
I wanna be your Ford Cortina
I will never rust
If you like your coffee hot
let me be your coffee pot
You call the shots
I wanna be yours

I wanna be your raincoat
for those frequent rainy days
I wanna be your dreamboat
when you want to sail away
Let me be your teddy bear
take me with you anywhere
I don't care
I wanna be yours

I wanna be your electric meter
I will not run out
I wanna be the electric heater
you'll get cold without
I wanna be your setting lotion
hold your hair in deep devotion
Deep as the deep Atlantic ocean
that's how deep is my devotion

*I wanna = I want to

5 Check your understanding.
1 A vacuum cleaner cleans up dust. What is 'dust'?
2 The metal on an old car rusts. What does the verb 'to rust' mean?
3 What does 'You call the shots' mean?
   a) 'You make the decisions.'
   b) 'You make a lot of noise.'
   c) 'You use a gun.'
4 What does 'I don't care' mean?
   a) 'I'm not happy.'
   b) 'It isn't important to me.'
   c) 'I'm bored.'
5 An electric meter 'runs out' when there is no money in it. What does 'run out' mean?

6 Answer the questions.
1 What is the rhyme scheme of the poem? Mark each line according to the rhyme of the last word, like this:

I wanna be your vacuum cleaner	A
breathing in your dust	B
I wanna be your Ford Cortina	A
I will never rust	B

2 How is the rhyme scheme of the last verse different? Why do you think the poet makes it different?
3 In verses 1 and 2, how are the last two lines different from the first six lines?

7 Read this extract from a magazine article and answer the questions.

John Cooper Clarke is sitting in his dressing room at a club in London. He's about to give a performance and he's talking to an interviewer, Ian Burns.

I started off writing in a band, The Vendettas, in the late sixties ... but punk helped because there was a lot happening. It gave me a lot of opportunities and it got me out of Manchester and around the world. But I've never felt myself to be part of any movement.

When I first started doing readings in the mid seventies there weren't really any poetry venues, there wasn't a poetry scene, so I performed at places like Mr Smith's, a club in Manchester, for an audience that probably didn't even read books. But poetry has always been and always will be a very different way of writing, a minority interest. It's language with its best suit on.

I suppose I am a comedian ... certainly when I play comedy clubs, I concentrate on the funny poems. But then last week I did a gig at the Birmingham Readers' and Writers' Association which was a literary event, so I did the slower, observational stuff.

Yeah, I read some of my poetry very fast ... that started with punk, really ... the high energy side of it. I thought, 'Right. I'll read them fast.' And it draws the audience in if they can't get all the words. It's like if you whisper into a microphone, then they'll stop talking and listen, because they feel excluded. If you shout 'Shut up!' then they'll just carry on.

1 John Cooper Clarke is a performance poet. What is a performance poet?
2 How did he start writing poetry?
3 How did the punk movement help him?
4 What kind of audiences did he read to?
5 What are his performances like?

What do you think?

▶ Is 'I wanna be yours' a typical love poem? What makes it different?
▶ Does John Cooper Clarke look like a typical poet? What type of person do you normally think writes poetry? Why?

PROJECT

Write another verse for the poem.

*I wanna be your mobile, baby
And whisper in your ear
_____ , maybe
_____ here.*

Read your verses aloud in class.

20 LITERATURE

Bram Stoker – Dracula

1 Read about Bram Stoker, the author of *Dracula*.

> Bram (short for Abraham) Stoker was born in Dublin, in Ireland, in 1847. After he finished his university studies there, he worked for the government, and married a Dublin girl who once nearly married Oscar Wilde. Like Wilde, Bram Stoker was very interested in the theatre. In 1878 he moved to London and became a theatre manager. He died in 1912.
>
> *Dracula* appeared in 1897. Stoker chose the setting of Transylvania because there were many stories about vampires in eastern Europe. The book is as popular today as it was a hundred years ago.

Why do you think *Dracula* is still popular?

2 Answer the questions about Dracula.
1. What is Dracula's full title?
2. What kind of place did he live in?
3. What did he look like?
4. What colour did he dress in?
5. What animal sound do you hear during the night in *Dracula* films and horror films generally?
6. What do you know about the story of *Dracula*?

3 Read the text. Which lines in the story make it seem frightening?

Jonathan Harker's Diary

1 Count Dracula

My story begins about seven years ago, in 1875. My name is Jonathan Harker, and I live and work in London. My job is to buy and sell houses for other people. One day, a letter arrived for me from a very rich man who lived in Transylvania. He wanted to buy a house in England and he needed my help. The man was Count Dracula, and I agreed to help him.

I found a house for him and he asked me to take all the papers for it to Transylvania. I was not very pleased about this. I was planning to get married in the autumn, and I did not want to leave my beautiful Mina.

'But you must go, Jonathan,' she said. 'The Count is rich, and perhaps he will give you more work later.'

So I agreed to go. I did not know then of the terrible danger which waited for me in Transylvania.

****

Soon we were on our way to Castle Dracula. The mountains were all around us and the moon was behind black clouds. I could see nothing – but I could still hear the wolves. The horses went faster and faster, and the driver laughed wildly.

Suddenly the carriage stopped. I opened the door and got out. At once the carriage drove away and I was alone in front of the dark, silent castle. I stood there, looking up at it, and slowly, the big wooden door opened. A tall man stood in front of me. His hair was white and he was dressed in black from head to foot.

'Come in, Mr Harker,' he said. 'I am Count Dracula.' He held out his hand and I took it. It was as cold as ice!

I went into the castle and the Count carefully locked the door behind me. He put the key into his pocket and turned to go upstairs. I followed him, and we came to a room where a wood fire burned brightly. In front of it there was a little table with food and drink on it. The Count asked me to sit down and eat, but he did not eat with me. Later, we sat and talked by the fire. His English was very good, and while we talked, I had time to look at him carefully. His face was very white, his ears were like the ears of a cat, and his teeth were strong like the teeth

4 Answer the questions, but be careful: the answers to five of them are *not* in the text.
1. How old is Jonathan Harker? *We don't know. The answer isn't in the text.*
2. Why did Count Dracula write to Jonathan Harker?
3. Who is Mina?
4. What time of day was it when Jonathan arrived at Castle Dracula?
5. What did the driver of the carriage look like?
6. What did Jonathan notice when he shook hands with Count Dracula?
7. Where did the Count take Jonathan?
8. Why didn't the Count eat with Jonathan?
9. Why were some of the rooms in the castle locked?
10. When did Jonathan see Count Dracula on the second day?
11. What did Count Dracula like most about the description of his new house?
12. Why did Count Dracula want a house in England?

Who? What? When? Where? Why? How?

5a Put the verbs into the correct places. Then check your answers by looking back at the text.

burned   laughed   locked   opened   stopped

1. The carriage *stopped* suddenly.
2. The driver ... wildly.
3. The door ... slowly.
4. He ... the door carefully.
5. The fire ... brightly.

5b Which adjectives can go with which nouns?

Adjectives	Nouns
strong	teeth
terrible	wall
tall	face
black	clouds
white	man
long	danger
high	fingers

strong man, strong fingers ...

What do you think?

▶ Look back at questions 1, 5, 8 and 9 in Exercise 4. What might the answers be?
▶ Why are horror stories popular?

PROJECT

Either:
Tell the same episode from Dracula's point of view. Start like this:
Good news from England. I have a house and Mr Jonathan Harker is on his way to tell me all about it.
   Aha, the doorbell! He's here! ...
Read your story to the class.
Or:
Find out about Dracula's Castle in Transylvania today and write a leaflet advertising it.
Come to Dracula's Castle! See the ...

of an animal. There was hair on his hands and his fingers were very long. When he touched me, I was afraid.

It was nearly morning when I went to bed, and outside, the wolves were still howling.

The next morning I found my breakfast on the little table in front of the fire. Now that it was light, I could see that Castle Dracula was old and dirty. I saw no servants all that day.

The Count did not come to breakfast, but there was a letter from him on the table.

'Go anywhere in the castle,' it said, 'but some of the rooms are locked. Do not try to go into these rooms.'

When the Count came back in the evening, he wanted to know all about his new house in England.

'Well,' I began, 'it's a very big house, old and dark, with a high wall all round it. There are trees everywhere. That's why the house is dark. It has a little church too.' And I showed him some pictures of it.

He was pleased about the church. 'Ah,' he said, 'so I shall be near the dead.'

Glossary

1 Countries in the UK

population number of people living in a country
official decided by the government
main most important
minority used by a smaller number of people
relaxing doing nothing, not working
medieval from the time between 1000 and 1500 AD
heart (of a city) the most important part in the centre
expect think that something will happen
surrounded by with … all around you

2 Great British Food

a takeaway a meal that you take out from the restaurant
ready meals meals that are already cooked for you
survey questions asked to many people
variations other ways of doing something
flour white powder used to make bread
sauce liquid that you put on food to make it nicer
pastry mixture of flour and butter, used to make pies
to cover to put on top
to grill to cook under a grill, with the fire above the food
manual jobs jobs that you do with your hands
stems the long part of a plant from which the leaves and flowers grow
special occasions for example, birthdays, weddings
dessert the sweet food you have at the end of a meal

3 Halloween

origins where something began
sacred/holy important for the church and religion
inhabitants the people who live in a place
supernatural things that can't be explained by the laws of science
creatures living animals
spirit part of a person that continues after death
relatives family members, e.g. brother, uncle, niece
to reflect to show, be an example of
scary frightening
dress up to wear special clothes
to flicker to start to die
to peel to take the outside part off an apple, orange etc.
harvest the time of year when farmers collect all the food
sunset when the sun goes down at the end of the day
an excuse a good reason to do or not to do something
fancy dress wearing special clothes so you look like a different person

4 Bonfire Night

festival a special time of year when people celebrate
midsummer the middle of the summer
enormous very big
event something that happened
gang a group of people, often planning to make trouble
gunpowder the powder that burns in guns and fireworks
to search to look for
enemy the opposite of friend

5 Christmas around the world

presents things that you give people for Christmas, birthdays etc.
pastries small cakes
relatives family members, e.g. brother, uncle, niece
carol a Christmas song
charity an organization that collects money to give to people that need it
Christmas stocking a bag in the shape of a foot
boxing the sport where people hit each other with their hands
to deliver to take to someone's house
neighbourhood the area around where you live
cool down to stop you feeling too hot
seafood shellfish and other food from the sea

backyard the area behind the house where you can sit or play games
sales when the shops sell things for less than the normal price
flip-flops type of shoe that you wear in summer, at the beach or pool
annual every year
sacks big bags to put things in
chimney the thing above the fire, where the smoke gets out of the house
brandy strong alcoholic drink made from wine

6 Hogmanay

gift something you give to someone, e.g. for a birthday
trading partners people you buy things from and sell things to
holy important for a church or religion
hearty strong, making you feel full of life
trusty someone you know will always be a friend
Viking the people from Scandinavia between 700 and 1000 AD
invaders people who go into another country to try and control it
warmth the opposite of cold
coin a piece of money made of metal, not paper
procession a line of people moving slowly through the streets
warship a ship that is used to fight a war
parades people walking through the streets, to be looked at
huge very big

7 Pantomime

comedy funny
Dame old-fashioned name for a woman
on stage where the actors stand in the theatre
comic funny
goes on continues
comedians people that make you laugh
silly stupid
put on (a pantomime) organize and prepare
join in not just watch, but take part in
fall over fall to the floor
invitation letter asking you to go to a party
a ball a big expensive party with dancing
accept say yes
coach the thing people sat in to travel, behind the horses
try on to wear something to see if it's too big or small
it fits it's not too big or too small

8 An English village

population the number of people that live in a place
inhabitants the people who live in a place
recreation enjoying yourself in your free time
thatched with a roof made of dry 'grass' on top
straw the dry part of wheat that animals sleep on
reeds tall plants that grow in the water
basic items the ordinary things you need to buy
to date from to come from a particular time

9 Two schools in India and Pakistan

Empire parts of the world under the control of one country
gain independence to become free to control yourself
rule control
official decided by the government
main most important
fairly quite
essential something that you really need
enrol to become a member
shifts the parts of the day or night when people can work
emphasizes says that this is very important
secular not connected with the church or religion
extra-curricular outside the normal school subjects
vital something that you can't live without
object the thing you want to do
opposing on the other side from you
arts and crafts painting and making things with your hands
debating discussing in a formal way what is right and wrong
to choose between to decide which one you want to use

10 February Festivals

religious believing in God and going to church
origins where something comes from
soldiers men who fight in the army
in secret without anyone knowing
variation a different way of doing something
violets blue flowers
reflecting showing
guess try to think of the answer when you don't know
keep in touch with not forget
an excuse a reason to do something that isn't necessary

11 A nice cup of tea

kettle the thing you use to make hot water when you make tea
awful very bad
indicator something that shows
minority a small part of the population
loose leaf tea tea that isn't in a tea bag
boiling at 100° centigrade
to taste so that it's the way you like it

mug a big cup
via going through this place on the way
trading post a place where people can buy and sell things
on sale possible to buy
alias or by its other name
took to started liking
taxes money you have to pay to the government
illegal against the law
overnight from one day to the next
to import to bring into the country
tea stocks all the tea that was ready to be used
warehouses the big buildings where things are kept before going to the shops
munitions guns and other things used by soldiers to fight

12 A walk through London

prison the place where criminals are kept
cells the rooms in a prison
to feed to give something to eat to
temple a church in some religions
to design to plan and draw how a building will be
appeared in played a part in
cannon a very big gun that shoots big balls
thatched roof top part of the building made of dry 'grass'
sculpture a work of art made in wood, metal, or stone
well worth seeing something you really should see
power station the place where people make electricity
views what you can see through the windows
items things
escalator moving stairs
smelling salts a bottle of liquid with a strong smell, used in the past to wake people up
brandy strong alcoholic drink made from wine
nervous worried and frightened

13 Robin Hood – England's most famous folk hero

brave not afraid of doing something dangerous
mention talk about
outlaw someone that lives outside the law
enforcing making it happen
monk religious man who lives in a special place
cheerful happy and positive
quick-witted very clever and intelligent
loyal always a friend
ballads songs
skill ability to do something well
versions different examples
Crusades the wars of Europeans trying to take back Jerusalem, from the 11th to the 13th centuries
evil very bad
raised made higher
arrested made him a prisoner
imprisoned put in prison

14 New Zealand

heavily populated with a lot of people living there
hissing making a noise like a snake
boiling at 100° centigrade
springs where water comes up from the ground
vast very big
location the place where a film is made
hiking walking in natural countryside
caving going into the big spaces under the ground
white water rafting sailing in rivers that go very fast
purpose reason why you do something
opposing on the other side from you
bankrupt with no more money
easy-going not difficult to live with
egalitarian seeing all people as the same
indigenous belonging to a place from the beginning
give up to give away to another person
the vote the ability to decide who will be in government

15 Roger McGough – *Mafia Cats*

entertaining interesting and enjoyable
accessible easy to understand
amusing funny
basis the thing which is the start of something
monk religious man who lives in a special place
in honour of saying how good someone is
tax money you have to pay to the government
insurance money you pay so that you get money when something bad happens
illegal against the law
pepperoni Italian sausage
keep a secret not tell other people something

16 Mark Twain – *The Adventures of Tom Sawyer*

based on written using the information from
main characters most important people in a book or film
brush the thing you use for painting
to obey to do what someone tells you to do
to break the rules to not do what society tells you to do
a fellow a man (old-fashioned)

17 Wendy Cope – Three poems

to peel to take the outside part off an orange, apple etc.
to share to give part of something you have to other people

contentment quiet happiness
list piece of paper with all the things you have to do
vegetarian person who doesn't eat meat
endangered when very few of a kind of animal are still living
at least this is one positive thing I can say
nervous afraid of what will happen
determined being very sure that you will do something difficult
get in touch with to learn more about something that has been forgotten

18 Oscar Wilde – *The Canterville Ghost*

to scare to frighten
hurried went as quickly as possible
a scream a loud shout by someone who is frightened
stomach where your food goes to in your body
crashed down came down very hard
roof the top part of a building
put on wear
went out stopped burning
go on and on not stop for a long time
turn into become

19 John Cooper Clarke – *I wanna be yours*

opening act the first person or group in a concert
to breathe in to take in air through your mouth and nose
dust the very small pieces that often need cleaning away in a room
to rust metal rusts when it gets wet and goes brown
to call the shots to be the one that decides what will happen
to sail away to leave in a boat or ship

to run out to not have anything left in it
deep devotion strong feelings of love
dressing room the room where people get ready before a concert
movement a group of artists with their own style
venues places where concerts happen
a minority interest something which interests only a small group of people
comedian person who makes people laugh
concentrate on to give most importance to
do a gig to give a concert
literary event when a group of writers come together to talk to the public
observational looking at people carefully to see what they do
draw the audience in make the people listen to you very carefully
to whisper to talk very quietly
feel excluded to feel that you don't belong
to carry on to continue

20 Bram Stoker – *Dracula*

setting the place where a story happens
vampires creatures like Dracula that drink blood
carriage the thing people sat in to travel, behind the horses
ice frozen water (at 0° centigrade)
wolves plural of wolf, a wild animal that looks like a dog
howling the noise made by wolves (often when the moon is shining)

OXFORD
UNIVERSITY PRESS

Great Clarendon Street, Oxford OX2 6DP

Oxford University Press is a department of the University of Oxford.
It furthers the University's objective of excellence in research, scholarship,
and education by publishing worldwide in

Oxford New York

Auckland Cape Town Dar es Salaam Hong Kong Karachi
Kuala Lumpur Madrid Melbourne Mexico City Nairobi
New Delhi Shanghai Taipei Toronto

With offices in

Argentina Austria Brazil Chile Czech Republic France Greece
Guatemala Hungary Italy Japan Poland Portugal Singapore
South Korea Switzerland Thailand Turkey Ukraine Vietnam

OXFORD and OXFORD ENGLISH are registered trade marks of
Oxford University Press in the UK and in certain other countries

© Oxford University Press 2009

The moral rights of the authors have been asserted

Database right Oxford University Press (maker)

First published 2009

2018 2017 2016
16 15 14 13 12 11

No unauthorized photocopying

All rights reserved. No part of this publication may be reproduced,
stored in a retrieval system, or transmitted, in any form or by any means,
without the prior permission in writing of Oxford University Press,
or as expressly permitted by law, or under terms agreed with the appropriate
reprographics rights organization. Enquiries concerning reproduction outside
the scope of the above should be sent to the ELT Rights Department, Oxford
University Press, at the address above

You must not circulate this book in any other binding or cover
and you must impose this same condition on any acquirer

Any websites referred to in this publication are in the public domain and
their addresses are provided by Oxford University Press for information only.
Oxford University Press disclaims any responsibility for the content

ISBN: 978 0 19 471102 9

Printed in China

ACKNOWLEDGEMENTS

The authors and publisher are grateful to those who have given permission to reproduce the following extracts and adaptations of copyright material: p32 'Mafia Cats' by Roger McGough from Bad Bad Cats (© Roger McGough 1997) is reproduced by permission of PFD (www.pfd.co.uk) on behalf of Roger McGough; pp34-35 from *Oxford Bookworms 1: The Adventures of Tom Sawyer* by Mark Twain, retold by Nick Bullard © Oxford University Press 2000. Reproduced by permission; pp36-37 'The Orange', 'Valentine', 'Kindness To Animals' from *Serious Concerns* by Wendy Cope. Published by Faber and Faber Ltd. Reproduced by permission; p38 from *Oxford Bookworms 2: The Canterville Ghost* by Oscar Wilde, retold by John Escott © Oxford University Press 2002. Reproduced by permission; p40 'I Wanna Be Yours' by John Cooper Clarke © John Cooper Clarke. Reproduced by kind permission of the poet; pp42-43 from *Oxford Bookworms 2: Dracula* by Bram Stoker, retold by Diane Mowat © Oxford University Press 2000. Reproduced by permission.

The publisher would like to thank the following for their kind permission to reproduce the following material: AKG-Images p22 (Saint Valentine observing a young couple, the origin of Valentine's Day. Hand-coloured woodcut of a 19th-century illustration/North Wind Picture Archives); Alamy Images pp6 (Steak and Kidney pie/Bon Appetit), 6 (Shepherd's pie/Tim Hill), 6 (Sausage and Mash/Tim Hill), 6 (Trifle/foodfolio), 18 (Pub sign/Alistair Laming), 18 (Barrington Cambridgeshire/Alistair Laming), 22 (Shrove Tuesday pancake race/Robert Estall photo agency), 24 (teaset/Tim Hill), 29 (Statue of Maid Marian and Robin Hood/John Robertson), 30 (Kiwi/Peter Arnold Inc.), 30 (Tuatara reptile/Peter Arnold Inc.), 30 (The Lion Peak, Fiordland National Park/Chad Ehlers), 33 (Kittens/Juniors Bildarchiv), 36 (Heart on tree/Caro), 40 (Water bottle/Payless Images Inc.), 40 (radiator/Oleksiy Maksymenko), 40 (1962 Ford Cortina/Motoring Picture Library), 42 (Dracula 1931/Photos 12); Ardea p17 (Panto character); Bridgeman Art Library Ltd p25 (Smugglers loading contraband on their ponies for the journey inland (litho), English School, (18th century) / Private Collection / Peter Newark Pictures); Britain on View p18 (Pub); Corbis p 34 (Tom Sawyer/Bettmann Archive NY); Getty Images pp16 (Pantomime), 25 (Porthole cuppa), 40 (Woman in raincoat/John Lund/Sam Diephuis); iStockphoto pp6 (Roast beef dinner/Joe Gough), 37 (Lamb/Eric Isselée), 37 (Barn Owl/Andrew Howe), 40 (Vacuum cleaner), 40 (Electric meter), 40 (Teddy bear/Marcin Krygier); Kendriya Vidyalaya School Delhi p 21; Link Picture Library p20 (Indian coffee bar); Mark Mason Studios p24 (mug of tea); Newspix Australia p 30 (Haka/Adam Head/News Ltd); OUP pp5 (Edinburgh Castle/Corbis), 5 (London Eye/Image Source), 5 (Roman Baths/Digital Vision), 5 (beach/Corel), 6 (Fish and chips/Stockbyte), 40 (Coffee maker), 40 (Shoal of fish/Corel); PA Photos p14 (Auld Lang Syne/David Giles/PA Archive); Photolibrary pp6 (Fried breakfast/Anthony Blake), 10 (Bonfire night/Nigel Francis/Robert Harding Travel), 12 (girl on beach/Juice Images), 36 (Girl smelling orange/Nugene Chiang/Asia Images), 40 (Man on sailing boat/Mats Widén/Johner); Rex Features p40 (John Cooper Clarke); Ronald Grant Archive pp16 (Aladdin pantomime poster), 28 (Robin Hood: Prince of Thieves (US 1991)); Tnimalan p 4 (coins); TopFoto pp15 (The First Foot: A Scottish custom on New Year's Eve 30 December 1882), 15 (Fireworks at Edinburgh Castle); Paul Wright p5 (Snowdon).

With special thanks to Muhammad Mohsin, p21 for the photograph of the Crescent Model School, Lahore.

Cover images courtesy: Carlos Butler (telephone box); Moi Cody (Stars and Stripes); Craig Jewell (cup of coffee); Elke Rohn (poppies); San San (film strip); Sophie/Quebec (Christmas decortation); Miguel Ugalde (rose); Steve Woods (bus); Michal Zacharzewski (leaf).

Illustrations by: David Atkinson/NB Illustration pp26-27 (Walk through London); Peter Bull pp inside front cover (map United Kingdom), frontis page (map Australia and New Zealand), 19 (Map of Barrington and duck), inside back cover (map USA and Canada); Paul Daviz/Illustration Agency p39 (Canterville Ghost); Fred Van Deelan/The Organisation pp 8-9(Halloween); Gavin Reece p13 (Christmas); Tony Sigley pp7 (food preparation); Lyn Stone pp10-11 (Guy Fawkes), 33 (Mafia Cats).